7 THINGS
YOU NEED TO KNOW
BEFORE LEAVING
HIGH SCHOOL

Preparing the next generation
for the next step

To: John.

NAPOLEON RICKS

PAGE PUBLISHING, INC.
New York, NY

First originally published by Page Publishing, Inc. 2017

ISBN 978-1-63568-875-7 (Paperback)
ISBN 978-1-64027-749-6 (Hard Cover)
ISBN 978-1-63568-876-4 (Digital)

Printed in the United States of America

DEDICATION

This book is dedicated to my teenagers and
all teenagers of the world

CONTENTS

INTRODUCTION

You are holding in your hands a collection of words arranged in a certain way to convey a very important message. These are mostly words that you already know and have heard, but the arrangement of them is done with a certain purpose in mind, and what you will read in this book may not be something that you have learned before but hope that, when you're done, it will not be something that you will easily forget. I am a believer in the power of words, both written and spoken, because most, if not all, of the changes you experience in your life will find its roots in something you heard or read. This is why it is super important that you guard yourself against the wrong words and position yourself to intake the words that support the life you desire.

> "Be as careful of the books you read, as the company you keep; for your habits and character will be as much influenced by the former as by the latter."
>
> —Paxton Hood

I hope that you will find the words written in this book useful and may they serve you as you develop great habits and form the character that will produce an amazing life. There are many valuable life lessons, powerful ideas, and useful tips in the pages of this book. I do not expect you to learn and apply them all at once, but what I hope you will do, is to pick up a couple of nuggets at a time and begin to apply them to your life. Then reread the book as often as you need to and on every read, pick up more gems. The more you read this book and practice the ideas put forth, the better I believe it will serve you.

CHAPTER 1

KNOW WHO YOU ARE

The age-old question "who am I?" is, in my estimation, the most important question you will ever be asked and, by far, has the most important consequence when you discover the answer to that question. The answer has the ability to propel you into a future of greatness that is reserved only for those who can make this all-important discovery. It will save you valuable time that will otherwise be spent in pursuits that are contradictory to the true you. Discovering who you are will also accelerate you toward fulfilling all your goals and dreams. It will inform you and direct you toward the people and place that best support that finding. It will stare you in a direction away from anything or anybody who could be counter-productive. Everything else that is going to be discussed in this book hinges on this chapter. This is why it's the first chapter in the book. I am convinced that if you fully comprehend what is discussed here and can follow the suggestions that I am going to be making, you will be well on your way to becoming all that you can be and living the life that most will only dream about. Let's get back to the question at hand. Who am I? Or who are you? As you attempt to answer that question, the first and most important thing you need to know is who you're not. The answer to that is a very simplistic one yet quite profound.

You are not anyone or everyone else. You are you, the only you, one in seven billion. You are unique in every way imaginable. There is no one else on this planet exactly like you nor has there ever been. You are physically unique that's why you are the only one that bear your fingerprints. You are uniquely gifted mentally, emotionally, psychologically, and spiritually and have been born with unique talents and abilities to fulfill a unique task. The sooner you accept this, the sooner you will be on your way to greatness. Your greatness lies in the discovery of who you are, why you are, what you are here to do and in doing it! If this was all you ever did in your time on this earth, you would have lived a great life.

I believe it was Tyler Perry who said, "Be yourself, because everyone else is taken." Trying to be someone other than who you are is to diminish your greatness. You are your most powerful when you are you. You have no equal or competition when you are being you. Stop trying to be someone else, because you will always lose at that game. Be yourself and you will always win because you are the best at being you.

Fish in the Water

Consider for a moment a fish. Fish belong in the water, and when it is in the place where it belongs, it dominates all other things that do not belong there that may try to compete with it. Man is no match for the fish as long as it remains in the water, so in order for us to have any power over the fish, we have to capture it by using tools and many forms of trickery to get it out of the place of its dominance. We understand that man versus fish in the water, fish wins. But if we can succeed in taking it out of the water, the fish will lose every time. The thought that I am trying to convey to you is that, once you discover who you are and operate in that realm, you will always come out successful. But if you follow the guile of other things that may seem attractive and leave the place of your power, you will never win. Life is about winning, not necessarily about winning against others but winning at being you, and the way to win is to figure out who you are and do it.

Fish must swim, birds must fly, singers must sing, doctors must heal, teachers must teach, entertainers must entertain, writers must write. What must you do? Find it out, embrace it, love it, make no excuses for it, and do it for therein lies your greatest joy, power, and fulfillment. Mark Twain once said that the two most important days in a man's life are the day he was born and the day he discovers why.

In order to get to the "why," you must first understand one simple but very important thing: "what." Without the "what," you will never get to the "why" because for every "what," there is a "why." What are you? You are a man or a woman. You are black, white, or any of the many races in our world today. You have certain skills and abilities that are unique to you and different from others, you have a love and passion for something unlike other people, your temperament and emotions are different from that of others, and you were brought up in a manner similar to but very different from other people. You have been dealt a hand in life that is uniquely yours, and it doesn't matter if you are rich or poor or what your social economic background is. All of this and more makes you what you are and should contribute when it comes to discovering why you are. One's most important discovery is the discovery of oneself.

Exposed to Your Future

I believe that we all have greatness within and that we are all geniuses in one way or the other. One way to ignite your genius and bring out the greatness from within is to be exposed to many different people, careers, professions, and talents. When you do this, you are giving yourself the opportunity to discover your greatness because, on that day that you meet someone or are exposed to something that you are uniquely designed to be and do, the real you will come to life, and on that day, your genius with be ignited. Like my friend Ron King said, "You can never aspire to what you are not exposed to." This is what school is designed to do. As you go through school, you are exposed to many different subjects and vast array of people either directly or indirectly, and in this process, you should somehow be able to discover your personal skills, abilities, and talents. For some, this will be enough, but for others, it might take a bit more. If you are a part of the others, it may take you being in the presence of greatness and watching first-hand the unfolding and exhibition of genius to awaken your genius. How did the kid who wanted to become a doctor decide that that was what he wanted to do with his life? He was more often than not exposed to doctors, and when he was, the genius within came to life, and on that day, he decided that no matter what it took, he was going to become a doctor. The same is true for everyone else and the same is also true for you. Whether you want to become a doctor or lawyer or actor, a race car driver, a professional athlete, a business professional, a carpenter, or a mother raising her kids at home, the best way to discover this is to be exposed to that way of life. If you at this point in your life still have no idea what you want to spend the rest of your life doing, I will encourage you to begin to expose yourself to as many different people and professional as possible. Follow the leading of your heart. It is pulling you to the direction of your genius. Go ahead spend some time with that mechanic, visit your local politician, talk with the chef at your favorite restaurant, volunteer to help the less fortunate, and I guarantee you that one day the "you" now will meet the "you" of tomorrow, and on that day, your genius will come alive and your future path will be firmly established. On the new Steve Harvey show, *Little Big Shot*, he showcases young geniuses, mostly kids under ten years old. One of the episodes, he featured a young talented piano player who was only three years old. When asked how he learned to play the piano, he said that his parents bought and brought home a piano and he just starting playing. Just like that—no lessons, no teacher. His genius came to life the moment he laid eyes on the piano. It happened for him, and it can likewise happen for you. All you need to do is be exposed to the greatness that is already in you.

Know That You Are Different

The value that you are as an individual is not found in your ability to identify with a group or to be like others. Your value is found in your ability to identify your unique difference and to develop it. That thought is antithetical to what you have probably been thinking. I know that as a teenager you have worked hard to look the part, act the apart, and even speak like your friends do. However, what I am endeavoring to teach you is that, if you will discover who you are and the greatness that is within you, you are going to have to do so not by trying to fit in but by being that individual who may in some instances be counter cultural. All the growth and progress that you are going to have will not come by you trying to identify with one group or another. It will come only by you spending time working on yourself and that thing that makes you different from everyone else. You are special not because you look like and dress like and talk like everyone else. You are special because you're different from everyone else.

Think about this for a moment: there are many companies that make cars but the reason why one would buy a particular make or a certain model is not because it is just like the others. A person choses one car over the other because it is different from all other cars.

Therefore, your value to the world is not in your ability to be exactly like your peers, but to the contrary, it is in your ability to distinguish yourself from the group. If you are selected for a job or a position on a sport's team or picked for anything for that matter, it will be because you have that differentiating quality that is sought after.

I am not a huge lover of hamburgers, and I don't take a moral or health position on why I don't eat it more than I do, but whenever I feel the need to have one, I always go for Burger King. There is something about the flame grilled whopper that does it for me. I have tried burger from just about every fast-food joint, but when I really want one, it has to be a whopper. I am sure that other people feel the same way about other burgers, but that still emphasizes my point, which again is that you are desired not for being the same but by being different. Imagine if all the burgers in the world were exactly the same. There will be no need for all of the verity that we have. The greatness of all the various taste is found in the fact that they taste different.

Know That You Solve a Problem

Everything in our world is made to solve a problem and that means even you. One way that you can discover yourself is by asking yourself what problem or problems you solve. What human need are you most passionate about? What would you like to change and make better about your world? What group of people do you want to help? What cause drives you the most? The answer may not come to right away, but the pursuit of it will begin a life-long discovery and revelation of your true self that otherwise may not be revealed. Many of your contemporaries who have not read this book may never begin their pursuit because they may never ask themselves those important questions. Therefore, you are a few steps ahead of the crowd just because you are being exposed to what is in this book.

Your eyes were made to see, cars were made to solve transportation problems, watches were made tell time, sports and movies were made to solve entertainment problems, clothes were made to solve nakedness problem, what I am attempting to convey to you is that all things are made to solve one problem or another. The quicker you discover the challenges you are here to help solve, the more you will avoid wasting time and the more fulfilling your life will be.

Below are eleven questions you need to ask yourself on this journey of self-discovery. I wrote this in another book and I think that they are appropriate for you to consider so I am sharing them with you here.

1.   What would you rather be doing?

Consider for a moment the work that you are doing right now or whatever it is that you are spending your time going. Could you say without second thought that you are doing exactly what you want to be doing for the rest of your life? If the answer is no, then there is something else in your heart and mind that you would rather be doing. Whatever that thing is, it may be your purpose trying to reconnect with you. So whether you like what you are doing or not, ask yourself if there is something that you would rather be doing. If the answer is yes, then you have an opportunity to follow that lead and see where it takes you.

2.   What do you have passion for?

We all have that burning desire to do something, be somewhere, or serve someone. You need to honestly ask yourself what that thing is that you are passionate about. Purpose always creates passion and this passion cannot be fulfilled by anything other than the thing that inspires it. When you have passion for a thing, just the mention of that thing causes your spirit to leap. It seems like every time you are around this thing, it puts a demand on your heart and draws you into a happy but uncomfortable place. You come alive and all the synapses in your brain seem to fire at once.

3. What could you do for the rest or your life even if you weren't getting paid for it?

If you were to asked anybody who is living according to their purpose and doing what they love whether they will still continue to do that if the money was taken away, their answer will be a resounding yes. And for those who are not yet making lots of money from doing what they love will tell you that they will do it for the rest of their lives even if the money never came. If asked why they do what they do, money may not even be mentioned on the list. The point I am trying to make is that the place of purpose is that place where you find fulfillment and contentment, and when you are in that place, the normal cares of this world do not matter as much. We all know that the pursuit of money is the number one goal of most people in our world today, but purpose is so powerful that even money loses its place when purpose is discovered. Contemplate on the following statement by Dr. Wayne Dyer: "When I chased after money, I never had enough. When I got my life on purpose and focused on giving of myself and everything that arrived into my life, then I was prosperous."

4. What are you good at?

Another way I found that will help you discover your purpose is to find out what you are good at doing. The reason this made the list is because I believe that when you were intended here, you came with a mission, and with that mission you were also given the natural mental and physical abilities to accomplish that goal. Usually, one's passion for a thing is associated with his or her ability to do that thing well. That's why doctors must be doctors, and carpenters must be carpenters, teachers must be teachers, and so on. I have never in my life dreamt of being a rocket scientist or a doctor or a lawyer. I was not given the tools to be any of that because they do not relate to my purpose. I love to help people. I love to speak. I love to write, hence the ability to do so. If you can find the answer, you will be on your way to discovering your purpose.

5.   Does it benefit others?

When you are moving in your purpose and doing the things that you are good at, do you find others being blessed or benefitting by what you do? Purpose is usually connected to others in some form or another. We are all given assignments that are unselfish and the reason for the gift is to serve and benefit others. Therefore, if you think you have a gift or a passion for something, one way to test if it is a divine calling is to see how it affects the lives of other.

6.   Does it inspire others?

There is a difference between inspiring others and blessing or benefitting them. When you bless someone, you bring something to them, but when you inspire, you bring something out of them. I remember Les Brown talking about the first time he heard Zig Ziglar speak. He was so inspired by him that he said to himself that he wanted to be like Mr. Ziglar. Zig Ziglar brought out of Les Brown what was already inside of him. He inspired him. Your purpose will do the same to others. It will awaken the giants that are asleep in them. How do people respond to you when you operate in your gift? That may be an indication of your purpose.

7. Does it inspire you?

"When you are inspired by some great purpose or some extraordinary project, all of your thoughts break their bonds. Your mind transcends limitations. Your consciousness expands in every direction. And you find yourself in a new, great wonderful world. Dormant forces, faculties and talents come alive and you discover yourself to be a greater person by far than you ever dreamed yourself to be." (Patanjali)

Another very powerful way to know your purpose is by how it inspires you when you operate in it. When one moves in their purpose, something happens on a spiritual level that cannot be duplicated otherwise. Supernatural forces come to your aid, your mind breaks its bonds, new ideas begin to flow. It almost seems as if you are connected to an inexhaustible energy source. At this place, you are most creative, you are really moving in the spirit. This is what Dr. Dyer calls being "in spirit."

I have had this happen to me many times as I operate in my purpose. You can ask anyone who lives in this place and they will tell you that something takes over their lives every time they move in their purpose. One experience was about five years ago. I went to Liberia to speak with college students. The first school that I spoke to was the African Methodist Episcopal University. About two hundred students came to the event, which was held in an outdoor auditorium in the middle of the day. I had prepared to speak for about an hour because I thought that, since this was a school environment and students had classes to attend, I would be speaking for no longer than an hour. I carried a notebook with a few bullet points on a particular topic that was sufficient for that time slot. Within forty-five minutes of the presentation, I had gone through all that I had to say, then something happened. Something took over. I felt a surge of energy that I didn't have previously. I began to say things that I hadn't prepared. the wisdom that came out of me was not my own. It was a hundred degrees outdoors. I was sweating profusely. All of my clothes were wet including my socks and shoes.

More students left their classes, and by the end of the presentation, the number had doubled. When it was all said and done, though soaking wet with sweat and haven spoken for about three hours, I felt totally energized. This is an example of what happens when you live in your purpose. It will inspire other people, but most of all, it will inspire you.

8.   Do others recognize it in you?

Whatever that "*it*" is for you is usually recognizable by others. The longer I live, the more I realize that the purposes that we all have are given by God to be used in the service of others. This is the most ingenious way to get the world to work in harmony. Unfortunately, we hardly live according to this divine blue print. Yet if we did, I believe that all our human problems will be solved. I don't know how I got off on that, but it came to me and I felt that it needed to be said.

Anyway, back to the matter at hand. Whenever you live according to your purpose, people will take notice and, in many instances, will bring it to your attention. Some of the most common ways they make that known to you is by the following:

- Have you ever considered doing that full time?
- You are a natural at that.
- Wow! That stuff just flows through you.
- You have quite a gift there.
- No one does it like you.

- I knew you had it in you.
- You should do that for the rest of your life.

These among many other ways people will bring to your awareness your purpose. As you seek to discover that purpose, do not neglect what others say about you but do not let that be the only determining factor for many have been told that they can't be or can't do and went on to be and do what others spoke against. The key to these methods is not to isolate one from the rest but to use them all together.

9.   Do you find yourself thinking about this all the time?

I do not know if there is a genetic predisposition as far your purpose is concerned but it can be argued that there is a spiritual and psychological leaning regarding one's purpose. This is the reason why I believe that when one is exposed to his purpose either in others or in him or herself, it triggers something inside. It strikes a chord and hit note that otherwise remains untouched.

Your purpose is that dream that stays with you when all others fade. It is that thing that you just can't get out of your mind, the one that you dream of night after night. It is who you are, it is what you are made to do, it is for that reason that you are wired the way you are. Because of your purpose, you were born into the family in which you were born. You are going through all the things you are and have gone through all that you have because of your purpose. It is the very breath that you take, it is the sight you see, it beats your heart, and it keeps you alive. You may have succeeded in locking it away in a dark room, but it is knocking and will continue to knock on that door until you let it out. It is in your mind right now; it is in your mind all the time. It is you, your very essence, the reason for which you showed up on this plane called "Life."

10. Do you experience your greatest joy and fulfillment when you do it?

Your greatest joy and fulfillment can only be found when you are operating in the place of your true self, in other words, in the place of your purpose. It really doesn't matter how grand or how low that place is. What matters is the joy that it brings you and how fulfilled you are when you do it. A person working at a homeless shelter serving tables in the place of his or her purpose is equally joyous as a famous actor operating in their place of purpose. For me, there is no greater joy and fulfillment than writing and speaking to people in an attempt to help them make better of their lives. What brings you your greatest joy and fulfillment?

Every time I step in front of people to speak, regardless of the size of the audience, I experience a sense of invincibility. It seems like I am one person, but as soon as I stand up and start speaking, someone else takes over. I am Clark Kent one minute, but the next minute, Superman shows up. Thoughts and ideas that I didn't originally think of start flowing. At that moment, I feel like I can do anything. When I am in this place, I hardly get tired. I remember a particular episode while speaking at a conference in India. I had been speaking to a large group of people for what seemed like an hour, but I actually spoke for three hours. The presentation went on so long that my host had to change interpreters. After three hours of standing and speaking, I felt energized and could have gone on longer. My interpreters, on the other hand, were completely exhausted. When you are in the place of purpose, you will feel unstoppable.

11. Can you live without it?

This final question was added to this list as a test of that purpose that you may discover through answering the ones that preceded it.

The real fact is that any purpose that is authentic is one that you will never be willing to give up, because living without this is equal to not living at all. To experience life on the level that it was intended to be lived, we all have to do so according to the reason for which we were placed here.

The flip side of this is if your answer is yes; maybe that discovery is not your real purpose. I will however encourage you to continue searching, for your purpose is discoverable but let this search start from within. There you will find all the answers you are looking for.

Now What?

Reread questions 1–11.
Then record your answers in the space provided.

_____

_____

_____

_____

_____

_____

_____

_____

_____

_____

_____

_____

_____

_____

_____

_____

Were you able to decide who the real you is? If so, wonderful! If not, keep reading. There is more to come to aid you in your discovery process.

CHAPTER 2

KNOW YOUR ENEMY

"When there is no enemy within,
the enemies outside cannot hurt you"

—African proverb

Once you have discovered who you are, the next thing is to know who your worst enemy is. Who is it that has the most power to stop or even hinder you from becoming who you want to become? Science teaches us that to every action there is an equal and opposite reaction. What that means in essence is that if your life is an action or a force, then there is something that acts contrary to that force or action, and the sooner you understand this truth, the sooner you can begin to address it. However, you need to also know that that force that works behind the scene, if you will, to contradict everything you do or attempt to do is not an external power. It is not something or someone outside of yourself that is trying to stop you from becoming what you want to become. Like the above proverb said, and I paraphrase, if the enemy within can't hurt or stop you, then the enemies without has no power to hurt you or stop you from accomplishing all that you purposed and set your mind to do.

Who then is your worst enemy? What I am about to reveal to you will shock some, surprise others, and leave many in disbelief. Here it goes. Your great enemy now and will always be *you*. You are the only one who has the power and ability to stop yourself from doing the things in life that you want to do and from becoming the person that you have imagine yourself to become. Fortunately, and sometimes when I think about it, it seems a bit unfortunate since you will never totally vanquish this enemy. It's fortunate and empowering to know this because by knowing this you reserve for yourself the ability to change your own life and to make it what you want it to be and not blame others or circumstances for your life not being what you desire. This means that you have the power and all you need to do is get out of your own way. Allow me to show you how to deal with this ever-present adversary and how to keep it at bay.

Take Full Responsibility for Your Life

From this moment forward, you need to begin to take full responsibility for everything that goes on in your life. The reason you pass or fail should not be someone else's fault. You do well or are mediocre not because someone did it. It's because you did it. When you make the right choice, or choose the wrong thing, it's no one's doing but your own. Every action you take is a choice that you made no matter the peer pressure, and the outcome and consequences of those choices is your responsibility. Own this. Embrace this for this is the place of power, the place where you decide to not give away your power to create the life that you desire. This is the place where you un-limit yourself, where you take off the shackles that hold you bond to others, societal stereotypes, and free yourself from social, economic, and racial limitations. At this place, you become the architect of your destiny, the creator of your fate, and the designer of the life you desire. The late great motivational speaker Zig Ziglar said, "You are designed for accomplishment, engineered for success, and endowed with the seed of greatness," but none of this will be realized if you refuse to take control of your life and continue to blame situations and circumstances or even others for the outcome of your life. Own your life, get out of your own way, and begin to win.

Believe in Yourself

"It does not matter how much people believe
in you. What matters is you believe in yourself."

A few years ago, my family and I visited a local water park here in New Jersey. It was a beautiful sunny summer afternoon. The park was crowed, the water was cool and refreshing, and everybody seemed to be having a great time. Over on side of the park, there was something going on that attracted a lot of people especial young kids, so naturally, I want to find out what was going on. I asked my wife to excuse me while I checked out the buzz. When I got there, I found out that there was a long line of people waiting anxiously to jump off a high cliff in a pond that was about twenty to thirty feet high. I watched as pre-teens and teenagers jumped one after another fearlessly off the cliff and into the water below. There weren't many adult doing this. I saw how much fun these kids were having as they came back for seconds and thirds and fourths so I decided to give it a try. I got in the very long line and inched my way closer and to my turn as one kid after another jump off the cliff with no hesitation. My heart pounded faster and faster with every step that I took, and the closer I got to the front of the line, the more I convinced myself that I was an idiot for wanting to try this. I began to imagine that I would die or break an arm or a leg or maybe even drown in the deep water because I was hardly a good swimmer. These thoughts and feeling grew stronger the closer I got to the front of the line, but I refused to turn back for fear of making a fool of myself in the presence of all these young people, so I braved it until it was my turn. It was my turn and I was called to step up to the edge of the cliff. As I slowly approached the edge, I told myself that I should have gotten out of the line when I had the chance. It would have been embarrassing then, but not as bad as it would be if I turned back now. I finally got to the edge and I looked over. At that moment, I realized how insane those kids are and how much more insane I am by allowing myself to want to do something this idiotic. Looking over the edge completely paralyzed me. My mind and body was in shock with fear but I had come way too far to turn back. I hesitated for a few more seconds, weighing the choices of turning back and disgracing myself or jumping and risking death. The anxious crowd began to chant, "Jump, jump, jump!" I heard people in the back of me saying "you can do it," "you can do it," and the guys at the bottom who just swam out of the water after their jump saying "jump, jump, jump." I finally decided to jump, choosing possible death over temporary embarrassment, so off the cliff I went. A split second later my body hit the water landing awkwardly causing much pain, but as I surfaced to the top of the water and swam to shore, the first thing I realized is that I was not dead. The next feeling that I had was one of exhilaration. I really enjoyed the jump, pain and all. It was great and I was glad that I did it. It felt freeing; it felt like, for a quick second, that I was flying. The landing hurt, but I finally convinced myself that I was a better swimmer than I gave myself credit for, so I went back and did it a few more times, and every other time that I did it, less fearful it was and the more enjoyable the experience.

The point that I am trying to make here by telling you that story is this: As I stood on the edge of the cliff and heard people tell me that they believe in me and that I could make the jump, I realized that nothing they say or think will make me jump off the cliff unless I take their "you can do it" and internalize it and turn it into "I can do it." I am not jumping off the cliff. You see what mattered is not that they believed in me; what mattered is that I believed in myself. What mattered is not what they said to me; what mattered is what I said to myself. What you think of yourself and what you say to yourself is infinitely more important than what everyone and anyone thinks of you. Therefore, if you can win the battle against your old self who wants you to only do the things that you have done, you will be well on your way to subduing your internal enemy.

The Most Important Conversation You Will Ever Have

Throughout your life, you have many conversations. Most will have no lasting impact but there will be a few that will change your life, and that change may last with you for a life. The things that others say and think of you, even the conversations that you have with others, can't have any impact on your life unless you internalize them and make them your own. Therefore, outside sources and forces have no power over you until you allow them. Take the previous story as an example, and by the way, one hundred percent of it is true. It really happened. As I stood at the edge of the cliff and heard people shout out to me "you can do it," it had no impact on me and could not move me to action until I took what they were saying and internalized it and turned their "you can do it" into "I can do." It was only at the point that I willed myself to move and take the dreadful leap. You see what matters is not what others think of you. What matters is what you think of yourself. What they say to you has no consequence on your life. What you say to yourself have the greatest repercussions. In order for me to convince myself that it was a good idea for me to take the leap, I had to tell myself that first and believe it also. All the things good or bad that have been said to you about you will not impact your life as much as the things that you say to yourself and believe. These are the things that will move you to action, the thing that will move you in the direction of your dreams, but if that talk that you are having with yourself are negative and defeating, then you are defeating yourself and stopping yourself from accomplishing and becoming all that you can be. I would have not jumped off the cliff if I did not win the internal battle and convinced myself that I could do it. If you win the internal battle of self-belief, no external enemy will ever be able to stop you from accomplishing your goals and dreams. So remember to always think positive about yourself and always affirm yourself because it the only conversation you will have on any given day that can affect your life. Consider the following quote: "He who believe he can't and he who believe he can are both right" (Albert Einstein). What matters here is what you believe.

The Greatest Hitter That Ever Lived

Eleven-year-old Sean is an avid baseball player and an enthusiastic fan of the game. He has a dream of one day playing in the major league. There is hardly a day that you will find Sean without something on him that is baseball related. He always had on a baseball cap or wore a baseball jersey, had baseball cards in his pocket, and was ever ready to play catch with his ball and glove in his backpack. One beautiful summer afternoon, Sean was in his backyard by himself, no one to play catch with so he proceeded to play by himself. Dressed up in full baseball attire with bat and ball in hand, Sean walked around the yard repeating to himself that he was the greatest hitter that ever lived. Sean then began to imagine that he was at an actual game and that he (the greatest hitter that ever lived) was up to bat. Because there was no one there to pitch him the ball, he pitched it to himself. So, as he imagined, he, Sean took the mound to pitch and he was also the hitter. With ball in one hand and his bat in the other, Sean wound up being the pitcher and the hitter. He gently tossed the ball high up in the air to give himself enough time to grab the bat with two hands and as the ball made its way down, he took a swing at it and missed it. "Strike one," he said. He then picked the ball up and continued to chant. "I am the greatest hitter that ever lived." He said this a few times, loud enough for others to hear him, returned to the plate, and got ready for the next pitch. The next pitch came in. He took another big swing at it, hoping to hit a grand slam for the bases were loaded and missed again. "Strike two," came the call from who else? Sean! You guessed it. He was also the ampere. He reached down, picked the ball back up, and again chanted that he was the greatest hitter that ever lived as he stepped away from the plate to gather himself. He returned to the plate, took a few practice swings, and pointed his bat to the outfield to signal that this was it. The last pitch was high, very high, giving Sean plenty of time to grab his bat and prepare for the swing. It came down right in the sweet exactly where he wanted it. In his mind, he said, "This is it." Sean swung at the ball with all his might and missed it yet another time. This time, he dropped his bat, took off his cap, picked up the ball, and ran around the yard, shouting, "I am the greatest pitcher that ever live! I am the greatest pitcher that ever lived!" According to Sean he was the greatest hitter that ever lived, and if this greatest hitter of all times was unable to hit his own pitch, then that must also make him the greatest pitcher that ever lived.

This is the exact attitude that I am trying to instill in you. You should never allow yourself to stand in your way or to defeat you, because if you are self-defeated, then you are truly defeated.

Never Settle, Never Stop Growing

Another important thing you must do in order to defeat the enemy within is to build and develop in you the attitude of never settling and to never stop growing. Always be on the move forward to a predetermine goal or future. There is always more to learn, more to accomplish, more to have. You can always be better than what you are right now, but you must desire it and take deliberate steps toward that end. Everything in our world is moving and changing whether you recognize it or not, even you. If that movement or change is not controlled and directed, it will move you in a direction or change you in a way that you did not intend. If you want this inevitable change to work in your favor, you are going to have to direct it by taking very intentional actions and making intentional choices to inform and guide it.

Never settle for failure, learn from it, do things differently, and overcome it. Never settle too long in your successes and victories. Celebrate it briefly, store it away for future reference, and move on to the next challenge. The purpose of failure is to teach you and expose your weaknesses. The purpose of success is to reward you for the hard work and to take you to the next step up the ladder. Both success and failure work hand in hand to prepare you for more challenging obstacles just ahead. Settling in any area of your life especially at this point in your life is selling yourself short of what you can be and accomplish. You can always grow and be better than what you are right now. Stay on the move. Always be on your way to somewhere or to something bigger and better than where you are.

Being Better Than Your Enemy

Being better than your enemy is being better than your best self: life is not about being better than others; it's about being better than who you were. If this is your goal, you will keep your enemy at bay and no one will be able to stop you from living the life you imagine.

If you are not where you want to be then where you are is not where you should be. Therefore, do what you have to do to get to where you want to be and, once you get there, set bigger goal and start the process all over again. Getting better is not doing the things that you are able to do or have mastered. Getting better is doing the things that you have not done and have not mastered. Getting better is stretching beyond your limits. It's living outside of your comfort zone. Defeating your enemy is constantly trying to be better than your previous best.

Understanding Self-Government

We are all created to be under some form of government, but the best form of government to be under is self-government. I believe that one of the reasons why there is a need for government as we know it is because of the lack of self- government. Part of the reason why school is important is to help you develop and maintain a level of independence, self-government, and maturity. The rigors of school starting with high school and even before high school and to college is to help you to establish the following characteristics:

- Self-discipline
- Self-leadership
- Focus

Self-discipline is the ability to set rules and boundaries for yourself because of goals and aspirations that you hope to accomplish and have. This is the most powerful kind of discipline because it is self-imposed and is motivated by goals that you set for yourself.

Those goals can range anywhere from getting a better grade on your next exam to running for office in your student government. A very important byproduct to this attitude is that it carries over to other aspects of your life. A friend once told me that the way you do anything is the way you do everything. Disciplining yourself now will lead to disciplining yourself later in life when it will matter most. Failure to discipline yourself now will have adverse repercussions.

Leaders are individuals who inspire others to follow them toward the achievement of a set goal. The ability to lead others begins with the practice of setting goals for yourself and motivating yourself to work toward the attainment of said goals. There is no place better than right now, where you are at this stage of your life, to begin to practice this very valuable attitude. Start by setting small attainable goals for yourself and begin to discipline yourself to stay the course until those goals are accomplished. Many times, it will mean forgoing some of the things that we did previously or even enjoyed doing, but if your goal is that important, nothing (especially not yourself) should be able to stop you from achieving it. After you have attained your goal, set even bigger goals and begin the process of working toward it. This practice will give you the ability to inform and direct your actions toward the accomplishment of your goals, and soon, you will be motivating, inspiring, and leading others because you have learned to lead yourself.

> You can't depend on your eyes when your imagination is out of focus. (Mark Twain)

At this stage in your life, your imagination is most active. There are so many things that you are imagining yourself being doing and having. The problem here is that with such an active imagination, there is usually a lack of focus. When you discover who you are and what you want to do with your life, all that is left to do now is to focus your time and energy on doing that. Remember that you can't be everything, but there is definitely something that you can be so focus your mind and actions on being that. Imagine yourself as that person and do what it takes to become the person that you see yourself as. The only thing that is standing in your way from becoming the person you imagine yourself to be is your ability or inability to focus on that and to do what is required to become that person. You are the only one who can stop you, but if you get out of your own way, nothing external will be able to stop you.

> Concentrate all your thoughts upon the work at hand. The sun's rays do not burn until brought to focus. (Alexander Graham Bell)

Now What?

Make a list of the areas in your life that need improvement. Then write down at least one way you can change what you have previously done in this area to something new and different you could do instead. Take one area of improvement at a time. Practice your new and improved change until it become a habit. Tweak your change as often as needed to get the outcome that you desire. Remember to be patient with yourself. It takes twenty-one days to form a new habit and sixty-six days before it becomes automatic.

> "In order to have what you never had, you have to do something you have never done." (Zig Ziglar)

CHAPTER 3

KNOW THAT IT IS BETTER TO DO IT RIGHT THE FIRST TIME

"Anything worth doing is better
if done right the first time"

Before I go on to explain that quote, allow me to tell you this story. A high school teacher came to class one day and brought with him an empty water container, one of the ones made for water coolers. Along with the container, he also brought many large stones, gravel, sand, and water. He then proceeded to fill the water bottle with the stones. When he could get no more stones in it, he turned and asked the class if it was at all possible to get anything else in the bottle. Just about all the class said no, with a few exceptions who really did not know what to think. After a short pause, the teacher took the gravel that he had brought and he began to pour them in the container. The gravel found spaces between the stones and made its way to the bottom of the container, filling in the gaps left between the stones until there was no more room to squeeze in another piece of gravel.

Again, the instructor asked the class if there was room in the bottle for anything else. This time, a few said no while the rest of the class hesitated to respond. Taking the sand he had brought, the teacher started slowly pouring it into the vessel. The sand gradually made its way between the stone and the gravel. It found spaces that were not filled and it began to occupy them, from the bottom up to the top until no more sand could go in. For the third time, the teacher asked his class if it was possible to get anything else in the container. This time, the class shouted collectively "YES, THE WATER!" So he took the water and started to pour it in. The water made its way pass the stones, pass the gravel, and even pass the sand. It found air-tight spaces among them and filled the container from the bottom up to the top. The teacher continued to pour the water in until it began to overflow.

Facing his students, and looking them squarely into their eyes, he asked what was the meaning of this experiment. Excitement grew in that small classroom, and it got louder and louder as the students shoot to their feet out of turn to give an explanation for what they had witnessed. Some put forward a scientific explanation, others give a mathematical meaning, others thought it was psychological, while a few passed it off as a trick question. When the teacher finally regained control of his class, he asked them to be seated and said, "The meaning of this experiment is not what you all think it is. What it simply means is…Wait, before I tell what," the teacher said, "I must ask you to continue reading the chapter and at the end of the chapter, I will tell you the real meaning of the experiment. However, I have to warn you not to skip these next few pages only to find out the answer. Reading through the chapter will help you appreciate the meaning of the experiment when it is disclosed. Better yet, stop here, do not read further, go find a few friends or family members, and explain the experiment to them and see what they think the meaning is. After doing that, come back and read the rest of the chapter. See you soon."

Welcome back.

Welcome back. I hope that you learned a thing or two from that little exercise. By the end of this chapter, you will be able to better understand the meaning of the experiment.

As you already know, the title of this chapter is "Doing It Right the First Time." The older I got, the more I began to realize that it is always advantageous to do things in the order that they were meant to be done. Order is a very important concept. Everything in our world follows an order. Take the earth's climate for example: Have you ever noticed that the changing seasons obey a specified pattern and never deviate from it? Winter always follows fall, and fall stays closely behind summer, and spring goes before summer. The system repeats itself over and over again without fail. If this beautiful balance was ever interrupted, we would have a serious problem on our hands. Following a simple yet very complex pattern creates harmony and allows the elements of nature to function in due time, eliminating chaos and providing a beautiful balance that makes life possible.

Leafless Trees

One late fall afternoon, I was driving along the highway with a friend of mine. We had driven for a couple of hours and still had a few more hours before getting to our destination. At this point, we were not saying much to each other so I had some time to think quietly to myself. As we drove on, I began to notice the trees lining our path. What struck me was something that we all have seen but haven't given much thought. I realize that most of the trees had no leaves on them. As I said, I have seen this many times before, but this day was different. I think the reason why it registered in my mind is because I was in the process of writing this chapter of this book.

I started to look more intently as we drove by. It seemed like the leafless trees stretched out its branches like hands and fingers raised up to the sky expecting something. They had their proverbial arms and fingers lifted up high toward the heavens waiting for the new season. As a high school student, you are in a particular season of your life. This season will soon come to an end, so you must begin to prepare yourself for the next one while you are still in this one. In the up-coming chapters, we will discuss in greater length the various seasons in your life. For now, let's get back to this business of leaf-less trees.

We all experience the fall season year after year. During this time, there seem to be no shortage of fallen leaves just about every-where you turn. Have you ever wondered why trees lose their leaves at this time of the year? Prior to this day, I really hadn't given it much thought. However, with the image and the thought fresh on my mind, I turn to my buddy and asked him if he knew why trees lose their leaves before winter. Without giving the question much thought, he answered with the most inspiring answer I have ever heard and kept right on driving. I was struck and amazed by his insight, but for him it was just a quick answer to a trivia question that didn't have much significance to him at the time, so he continued to pay attention to the road. Meanwhile, I was bubbling inside and all over because what he said was so inspiring, and it made all the sense in the world, even though it wasn't a deep scientific answer. Okay, this was what he said, "So that they don't fall." I said, "What?" and he went on to say that he believes that trees lose their leaves before winter so that when the snow comes, it will have no leaves to rest on thereby preventing the tree from falling under the weight of the snow.

Think about that for a minute. Even the trees obey the order they are in, and they make adjustment to avoid chaos, destruction, and calamity.

Your Next Step

As you prepare to take the next few steps in your life, think about the order that you should follow, think about the things that you need to do that will prepare you for the next season of your life. Your life should obey a certain predetermined pattern, one that you have laid out that will help you stay on course, avoid mishaps, and prepare you for an expected future. A very simple plan may look a little something like this:

- Finish high school
- Go to college
- Finish college
- Get a job (pursue your dreams)
- Start a family

This plan is a very simplistic one, but you may be saying to yourself that life is more complicated than that. I understand that; however, if you make this simple plan your goal, you may be able to complete it with fewer complications. As I studied the lives of teens and late teens in this culture and in many parts of the world that I have been, it seems that somehow, somewhere between steps one and two, the process gets all mixed up. You see, this list can be one of priorities. When getting a job for instance takes priority over finishing college, it confuses the system. In some cases, getting a job is needed to facilitate going to and finishing college, but if this is something that can be avoided, by all means avoid it. You will be able to make much more money after you've successfully completed the first three stages.

Another very common example is moving stage five to stage one or two, or somewhere in between. If you are in high school right now and are reading this book, I can bet that you are saying to yourself, "I'm not trying to start a family." That may be true in the technical sense of the statement, but in essence, it is what you do when a relationship absorbs all of your time, emotion, and mental energy. When this happens in your life, it upsets the order, confuses you, and prevents you from making your best decisions. Therefore, the closer you stay with the process, the higher the chances for a better outcome.

It is when you refuse to follow a predetermined order that you find yourself in a heap of problems. Some of those problems can be easily overcome with a short recovery time while others have life-long repercussions. If you are reading this book right now and you are in middle school or high school, consider for a moment the order that your life had to follow to get you to where you are right now at this very moment. You have traveled through several stages of life already. You were born, you have gone through infancy, and you were once a toddler. You went to preschool, kindergarten, and so on. Through that process you have successfully made it to where you are, going from one stage to the next, not skipping any stage and not mixing them up. The next few steps of your life should follow the same pattern if you want to assure harmony, balance, and success.

The Teenage Dilemma

The only explanation I can possibly come up with for this is that, at the teenage stage of life, you begin to have the same physical appearance as an adult, you begin to feel like an adult, but without the adult's mind and without the adult's responsibilities. It is like having this awesome super power but lacking the knowledge of what it is intended for or how to even begin to unwrap it or use it.

I am reminded of my daughter Chayil. When she was a toddler and could move around the house, she quickly discovered the power and volume buttons on the television set. I was constantly using the remote to adjust the sound or turn the television back on because Chayil had a way of turning the volume up too high or down too low or turning the set off completely. With her, there was no medium. This is precisely what I see a lot of teenagers do with their new-found power. There seems to be no medium. It's all or nothing. When you let another teenager get a hold of your volume or power buttons, they are either turning it up too high or down too low. In some cases, tragically, they may turn it off. This proverbial button can represent your affection, your hope, your dreams, your zest for life, or even that thing that makes you who you are.

It is said that "youth is a marvelous period of life. What a pity so many don't know what to do with it." Every time I see a young man or a young woman abusing their youth, it breaks my heart. What I see is an individual with lots of potentials, a promising future, who doesn't realize how awesome and unique they are. It is really a sad commentary to say that great talents and potentials in our young people will go unrealized. The purpose of this book is to help save a few.

Lincoln in a Rock

I heard a story some time ago about a sculptor who had brought into his workshop a large rock and began to carve away at it. Every night he would have his maid come in and clean up the mess that he had made during the day. Day after day, as she did her work, she would wonder to herself what it was that artist was trying to make. The project took many days, and every time she came in to work, she saw the rock take shape, but it still puzzled her. One night after many days of the same routine, the maid came to work and found the rock covered. She was tempted to sneak a peek under the covering to find out what had become of the rock, but did not do so because she thought that if it was for her eyes, the artist would have left it uncovered. That night, the maid did her work as usual and went home. The next day she came to work a few hours earlier, hoping to meet her boss working on the rock. When she walked into the room, the master sculptor was doing the finishing touches on his master piece. To her greatest amazement, it was a sculpture of President Abraham Lincoln. Still totally in awe of the stunning artwork she walked over and tapped the artist on his shoulder and said softly, "I am sorry to disturb you, sir, but how did you know that President Lincoln was in that rock?"

Most of the time, when others look at you, all they see is a good-for-nothing rock. Sometimes, all you see in yourself is a useless piece of mass. I have had the opportunity to travel and speak to young people in several countries. I have been to India, Africa, Central American, and many parts of North America. Everywhere I go, I see young men and women teeming with life, hope, and dreams—potentials that are yet to be discovered. As you read these next words, I want you to realize that I wrote this book just for you. I wrote it just to let you know that inside this rock that everybody sees is a person, a gift, a dream, a masterpiece that is being shaped, and in due time, you will come to your fullness. If nobody else believes it, I do and you should too. I know that deep inside of all that unfinished work, there is a master sculpture that will amaze the world when it is finally completed and revealed.

Tune Up Your Instrument

"Do not have your concert first and
tune your instrument afterward." (James Taylor)

The admonition here that must be heeded is that beautiful music can only come from finely tuned instruments that were pretuned before the concert started. How does that apply to you? Your life is an instrument that should make great sound when it is played. To achieve the harmony and melody that is required to produce a grand concert, there has to be a certain level of preparation, which, for the sake of this metaphor, we will call tuning.

Take the guitar for example. Each string on the guitar has to have a particular amount of tension for it to make the right sound. When all the strings are properly tuned, the instrument produces a clean, crisp sound. Many times, the rigors of life, which will constitute school, homework, tests, and exams, are the tools that are used to produce the tension or balance needed for your life to bring forth wonderful music. As you move through life, tuning will continue, but the tools will change. Allowing yourself to be adjusted at every stage of your life beginning now will provide for you a future that few enjoy.

When Is the Concert?

Today is not the day for your concert. While you are still in school, while you still have a lot of academic work to do, today is the day that you tune up your instrument. Now is the time that you set your priorities, set the order that you want your life follow. Major in the major things, and let the minor things come after. Do not allow the time you spend on the telephone to take the place of studying and reading. Invest more in your classroom performance and less in peer acceptance. Let the accomplishment of your educational goals have more value to you than the opinion of others. Try your outmost best to dress your mind more than you dress your body.

I haven't been out of high school that long, but I can still remember how devastated we were to get a "C" on a test or homework, much less an overall average. Unfortunately, pop culture has hijacked the hearts and minds of so many young people that having the latest outfit and knowing the latest music seem to have more weight than achieving passing grades. The corridors of school that were once occupied by future leaders are now fashion runways. The classrooms are now used for everything other than learning.

I am privileged to have several nieces, two of which I am very fond of. The reason I am the way I am with them is because I have spent a lot of time with them watching them grow. They are Jelina and Loren. The both of them played a significant role in inspiring me to write this book. Whenever I had the opportunity to be with them, I tried to drill this message into their hearts. The simple message is that there is a day for their concert, but today is not that day. I would tell them that that day is sure to come and that they already have admission to the event. However, the grandeur of the event depends on them. It can be as big or as small as they want it to be. How that day turns out is completely up to them, but what they should not forget, is that their day is not today. Once things are done the way they are meant to be done, their day will be a major success and they would receive a standing ovation. This is true for Jelina and Loren and for you reading this book.

Yeah, But There Is Always a Second Chance

It is impossible to win in life if you
are always playing catch-up.

—Tiger Woods

As true as that statement may be, it does not hold in all areas of life. Your chances at being a teenager twice are equal to your chances at reliving the last twenty-four hours of your life. You only get one chance to get it right or else you will find yourself playing catch-up.

I played basketball for a good portion of my youth life, and during that time, I had a lot of memorable victories and heart-breaking loses. One defeat I will never forget is an intervarsity final game in which my team was clearly the favorite. I went to an all-boys Catholic high school where the competition was really stiff both academically and athletically. Every year, our school was historically favored to win it all or at least make it to the finals. This rich heritage of excellence and championships rested quite heavily on me and my teammates' shoulders as we rose to the occasion in 1991. I remember the year very well. I was a junior that year, and I had been starting more frequently for the best part of that season.

Wulwyn Porte, my good friend, was a senior, the captain of the team, and our go-to guy. I was sort of like the second option. Anyway, 1991 was a great year for our team. We had just come out from the inter-Catholic meet where we emerged champs. We had also qualified for another championship game scheduled for later that year, but the intervarsity tournament was the most desired and toughest of them all. As expected, we went right through the preliminaries. We had some very close games in the second round, tougher still in the playoffs, but through it all, we once again found ourselves top seed going into the finals.

On the other hand, the team that was challenging us for the crown was one that nobody expected to even be in this far. So going into this game, everyone knew what the outcome would be, St. Patrick's champions once again. Because we were highly favored to win it all, we did not take care to prepare for our opponent. We went into the game thinking that it was going to be a walk in the park, breakout the bubbly, hand us the trophy, and call it a night.

The game was anything but a leisurely stroll. Early in the match, we found ourselves down by a huge margin and faced with an opponent that was well prepared. They knew our strategies and were gunning for the kill. Throughout the game we struggled to dig ourselves out of the large hole the other team had dug for us. We played our best basketball that day. Our coach pulled out all the stunts, and because we were the more experienced and better-coached team, we were able to recover from the deficit, but not enough to win the game. Time ran out on us. If we had one minute more, we would have won the game. We lost not because of the lack of talent, for we had plenty, not because of the lack of experience, not because of the lack of good coaching, but we lost because we did not have sufficient time to recover from the deficit. We lost because we were playing catch-up or, in other words, we were playing from behind.

Zig Ziglar said that we are all engineered for accomplishment, designed for success, and endowed with the seeds of greatness. This statement holds true for you also, but as true as it is, it can only be actualized with preparation, hard work, and making sure you stay ahead in the proverbial game of life.

I Can Fix It If It Breaks

You might be saying to yourself, yeah, but I can fix it if it breaks. How about all the other people who made some terrible mistakes and still ended up successful? Again, I that hope you are not thinking this way because I trust that you are too smart to let that even be a consideration. Life is not an experiment; it is not a dressed rehearsal. This is the real deal. Some ills in life leave scars that last a lifetime while others are irreparable. So before you decide to go that route, I suggest you talk to a few people who tried to get it back together after a mess-up.

Talk to that young lady who had the lofty dreams about doing great things with her life after she got her education and a good-paying job. Let her tell you about her desire to travel and see that world, asked her about how much she wanted to sing and dance. Listen as she described her dream home to you, the one with the three-car garage and the pool in the backyard. Feel her pain as she tells you how those dreams were short-circuited because of an unplanned pregnancy. She was in love and her life was for a time defined by her relationship. It consumed all her time, energy, and passion. The relationship came to an end, but it left her with a baby. Now she has a wonderful child that she loves and will go to the ends of the world for, but at the same token, it has cost her the things that she dreamt about. She still carries those dreams in her heart and they are accomplishable, but the road to their reality is ten times rougher. As hard as it was to get an education, now it is even harder with a child to raise and a job to keep. To earn more money, she needs more education. To get more of that, she has to go back to school. How can she do that being a single mother who is committed to her dreams as well as the well-being and provision of her child?

Before you skip another class, talk to that middle-age person who had it going on in high school. Let him tell about how popular he was. How all the girls wanted to be with him and all the guys wanted to be him. He was the life of the party. As a matter of fact, there was no party without him. Wherever he was that's where the party was. Everybody wanted to be his friend. He was so cool that he thought that studying, home work, and getting good grades was for geeks. Now he's middle aged and is not as hip as he used to be. The girls don't want to be with him anymore and the guys don't want to be him. There are no more parties, no more accolades, no more friends. He is now trying to make sense of the only life that he has, so he is working for minimum wages and can't seem to make ends meet. Today he regrets every day of every minute of every class that he did not take seriously. He wishes that he could go back and do it all over again but it's too late. Talk to him. Let him tell you how important it is to do things right the first time around.

The Meaning of the Experiment

"The tragedy of the world is that man has given first class loyalty to second class causes, and these causes have betrayed them."

—Lynn Harold Hough

It is only fitting at this point for me to tell you the actual moral of the experiment involving the teacher and his class as related to you from the start of this chapter. Many explanations can be given to the exercise, but this one is the most appropriate, given the purpose for this book.

Let's go back for a moment and remember the experiment. You recall that the teacher brought to class an empty water container, some rocks, gravel, sand, and water, right? Good. He proceeded to put the rocks in first, then followed that up with the gravel, then the sand, and finally the water. Through this process, the teacher was able to get all the elements into the bottle.

The moral of the story is that you need to get the big things in first. This is the way life works. This is the way your life should work. Had the teacher started the experiment by putting the other substances into the container before the rocks, he would have had a real challenge getting the rocks in. By putting the big things in first, he managed to get a lot of the little ones in also. Stop for a minute and let that sizzle in our mind. Life will work beautifully for you if you just do the first things first, if you major in the major things, and give your first-class loyalty to first-class causes. Get the rocks in first—for example, your education, your career, your dreams whatever they may be, then follow it up with the things that may represent the gravel in your life, then the things you consider to be the sand, then the water.

Life is difficult as it is without the extra complication. Do not make it more difficult for yourself by not sticking with the system. By staying with the plan, you can eliminate a lot of the pressures and allow your time on this earth to be less stressful, much smoother, and more successful.

You have been given a huge responsibility, which is your life and the outcome of your life is up to you. The older you get, the more that responsibility becomes totally yours. In the last chapter of this book, we will explore that concept in depth, but for now I want you to know that this complex situation can be managed if you stay focused and take first things first.

The next quotation captures the heart of this chapter and is a fitting way to bring it to a close. I hope it brings it all together for you.

> "The older I get, the more wisdom I find in the ancient rule of taking first things first—a process which often reduces the most complex human problems to manageable proportions."

> —Dwight D Eisenhower

Now What?

Now that you know what you must know before leaving high school, what you need to do is as follows:

- Determine the things that are most important to you.
- Make sure those things hold some guarantees for a prosperous future.
- Write them down.
- Make a list of the benefits those things bring.
- Make a commitment to yourself and someone in authority over you to completing those things.
- Make a list of the secondary things in your life.
- Always keep these two lists handy and see to it that the secondary things never take priority over the primary things.

CHAPTER 4

KNOW THAT YOU DO NOT WIN JUST BECAUSE YOU SHOWED UP

"Everything comes to him who
hustles while he waits."

—Thomas Edison

My niece Loren is a phenomenal basketball player. She was the best player in her school; she's like a miniature Michael Jordan. One summer she played on two different teams in two separate leagues. In each tournament, her team went to the finals; they lost one and won the other. Loren scored more points than any other player in both leagues.

I remember the Sunday afternoon she had come home from the championship game, which they won. She was very excited about her accomplishments. I asked her if she was given a most valuable player award for her success and she said no. She then pulled out a medal and reluctantly said, "They give us this." Holding it in my hand, looking it over, I asked, "What is this? Is this what you guys played so hard for all summer? This is not a championship medal."

"No," Loren said. "It's the same medal given to all players on the team. I don't get a most valuable player award. We all get medals because my coach said that it is not good to make that kind of distinction."

It is unfortunate that this mindset is getting increasingly common in schools. The truth is that in life there will always be a greater reward for those who do more. You are not guaranteed the same reward just for showing up. You will have to decide if you are in this to win it or not. The medals of life are reserved only for those who win.

Like my niece Loren, most young people are familiar with either athletic competition or some other type of team competition. When two teams set out to compete in sports or any game for that matter, the one thing on either team's mind is winning. No one goes into contest to lose; every one entering the game wants to win. Winning is the object, it is the reason why you play, it is the ultimate desired outcome, and it is the only thing that totally satisfies the effort given.

Now that you are in the game called life, now that you have put on all the equipment and the jersey, are you in this to win it or are you here just to break a sweat and have a fun time doing it? I need you to make a decision right here, right now before you read any further, because what follows is only for those who want the ultimate prize. Are you in this to win it? If your answer is *yes*, say it a few times to yourself. Good. Let's go.

The Ultimate Prize

You may be in a classroom with many other students, and for now, you have to take the same lessons, the same test, and do the same projects. However, each person's ultimate prize at the end of the day will be completely different from the next. Even though you are all competing to win, you are not competing against each other. You are competing with yourself for the prize that you have set as your ultimate goal. My question to you at this point is, what do you want? What do you want the outcome to be? What do you ultimately want to achieve? No one can answer that question but you. You have to decide what you want. You have to own it. You have to want it so badly that you will go the distance to ensure that you get it.

Some time ago, I had a heart-to-heart talk with my other niece Jelina. She asked me to give her a ride from her job so I did. Since the ride would be about thirty minutes, I knew that it would be a good time to talk to her without distractions. Anyway, I picked her up. I started to talk but I could tell from her body language that she didn't want to listen, but it was my car so I had the right to talk as much as I wanted. She had no choice but to listen to me rattle on for thirty minutes. For the duration of the ride, Jelina was my captive audience.

With her permission, allow me to create for you the back drop to our conversation. Jelina was a sophomore in high school and her grades hadn't been the best. She was very disenchanted with the whole idea of school. She had been hearing it from her mom and dad, and the last thing she wanted was another lecture from me.

However, this young lady is a very talented singer. She spends a lot of her time singing and listening to music. All of her friends know her for that. Jelina, however, will not sing in public, except for when she was a little younger I used to make her sing along with me in church while I played the guitar. Even then she was special. Armed with this valuable information, I asked her, "What do you want to do with your life?" Without hesitation, she said, "I want to be a singer." She went on to tell me that she wanted to sing and write songs and perform and become a huge musical icon. I let her finish her thought then I began to tell her about the ultimate prize. I told her what I just told you, that no one can determine that prize. I told her that she had to own it. I went on to tell her that she should want it bad enough to do what it takes to acquire it. Then I added, "Do not apologize for it and do not make excuses for not doing it."

The ride ended up being a pleasant one, and we were both glad that we had our little talk. When we got to her mother's office (my sister Linda), she just finished talking to Ms. Janet, the receptionist, about how good of a singer Jelina is. Naturally, when we walked in the door, Linda asked Jelina to sing a song for Ms. Janet. Remember now, JJ, as we call her, does not like to sing in front of people so clearly she refused. Her mother kept pressuring her until someone else came into the office. This time JJ more strongly said no, even refusing to accept a financial compensation from her mother.

At that point I looked her in her face and said, "No excuses." I reminded her that when it came to the ultimate prize, she is not to make excuses. Upon that reminder, she sang a beautiful song by Alicia Keys, releasing a vocal talent that icons are made of. At the end of her rendition, the gentleman that walked in gave her five dollars and her mother promised to give another five bucks. In a matter of minutes, she made ten dollars. I turned to her and said, "At this rate, you will be a millionaire in no time and I'll be your manager."

Find Our Own Flame

Along with everything else that I have done, I was also an insurance agent. As an insurance agent, every four years, we had to complete a certain number of continual education classes in order to keep our licenses current. In one of those classes, I met a gentleman named Michael Obrien who happened to also be a high school math teacher. Michael was working on his master's degree at the time and was writing his master's thesis on the changes that need to take place in secondary education. Mr. Obrien worked at a high school in a town called Watchung Hills in New Jersey. I have never been to Watchung Hills, but Michael tells me that it is an affluent community. He said that most of the students in the school that he worked in did not have to go to school if they didn't want to. Their parents had enough money to take care of them for the rest of their lives. Knowing this, he said, some of those students will not take their education seriously.

If you are reading this book and you find yourself in such a position, there is something I want you to know. I believe that we all have an internal flame. Every individual has that thing in life that ignites passion inside of them. We all have that one thing that causes our hearts to beat faster when we see it in other people or when we do it ourselves. It is the thing that you do that captures all your attention. When involved in it, it seems like time comes to a standstill. Things as natural as eating and drinking become interruptions when you are in this zone. This is that thing that I call your flame. I call it your flame because it sets your world on fire. It is that deeply rooted desire that has always been with you. You do not remember when it started, you cannot get rid of it, and it brings you the most joy.

This flame may not be that of your parents, nor might it be the path they want you to take. As a matter of fact, it may even be the one thing that they don't want for you. The reason why you should take your life and your education seriously is because of that flame. It is because you have this burning desire to be and to become what drives you, day and night. No amount of money can replace it and no one else can do it. It has to be you. One of the benefits of having wealthy parents is you can use that wealth to get you to where you want to go. But you have to first know where that is and you have to want it for yourself more then they want it for you.

The thing that drives a successful life is not money or the desire for it. A successful life is driven by the discovery of the flame and the longing to see it come to reality.

The Flip Side

The flip side of this is like the other side of the same coin. The problem that Mr. Obrien faces with his students is not at all unique to them. The disenchantment that high school students have with school cuts across economic, racial, and cultural barriers. From the poorest communities to the richest, students are becoming more and more reluctant to fully apply themselves academically.

I am not going to pretend to be an expert on this matter, but there is one thing that I do know; and I discovered this by studying the lives of successful people of the past and those of our day. It does not matter who you are in terms of your race, financial back ground, or your cultural heritage. You can be successful if you only find out what that thing is that ignites the fire of your soul and spend the rest of your life doing it. Therefore, if you are thinking to yourself "I am not from a wealthy family so I can't do and have the things that the rich can" you are wrong. All you need to do is find your flame, fan it, develop it, nurture it, protect it, and pursue it and it will give you all the joys, fulfillment and prosperities that life has to offer.

Where does high school fit in all this

When I was high school and had to do math, and science, and learn the periodic chart, (I mentioned that because it made no sense to me back then and in many ways, still does not and it really upset me that I had learn something that did not directly apply to my life) I asked the same question. Where does this stuff fit in the greater scheme of my adolescent life?

The real truth is that it does. I have come to believe that education is designed to make you think. Its purpose is to put you through a rigorous process that flexes your mental muscles. In this process of mental weight lifting if you will, you develop the ability to constructively think in various ways and the end result is you are wiser then when you started. High school also allows you to experience or test drive many careers in order for you to find which one fits for you. It may not seem to have any value to you right now but trust me it is the first and very important step to the rest of your life.

No more church for me

I read a story some time ago that is parallel to what we just discussed. The story is about a grandfather and his grandson.

After the loss of his parents to a freak accident, George came to live with his grandfather. His grandpa lived on the top of a hill. He was a coal miner and was faithful in his church attendance. Because George now lived with his grandpa, he was compelled to go to church with him three times weekly. When his parents were alive, he did not have to go to church as much, so going three times a week was a stretch for him. George loved his grandfather very much and did not want to hurt his feelings because he knew what church meant to him.

Before George, Grandpa went to church all the time with Grandma. It was something that they both enjoyed together. When she passed, Grandpa continued the tradition because it was the one of the ways he felt close to his departed wife, and being in church helped him to cope with Grandma's absence. George being there was a great joy for his grandfather and he loved his grandson very much. Nowadays, Grandpa seemed to walk a little faster. He seemed to have regained a little pep in his step. Since his grandson moved in, he began to sing around the house. He started to smile a lot and it appeared as if he was finally going back to being the fun-loving grandfather he once was. One of his greatest joys was going to church with his grandson.

George, on the other hand, was growing wary of church all the time. He felt like the preaching was over his head. He felt he wasn't getting anything out of it and that the experience was a waste of his time. To make to situation worst, none of his friends went to church as much as he did. He tried to hint to his granddad that three times a week was a little too much but he saw how much grandpa loved it and wanted him there, and didn't want to spoil that for him.

George's frustration grew deeper and deeper as the weeks went by. He got to the point that he had to say something to his grandfather. One Sunday afternoon George went up to his grandfather's room and asked if he could talk to him about something very important. Granddad sat up on the edge of his bed and said, "Sure, George, what is it?" With much hesitation George said, "Let me get right to it. Grandpa, why do I have to go to church with you three times a week?"

"What do you mean, son?" Grandpa asked.

"What I mean to say is that we, I go to church with you three times a week but I am not getting anything out of it. I am not learning much, I feel out of place, and most of all I don't see any changes in my life at all."

George's grandfather thought about what his grandson had said and he came up with the most ingenious way to resolve the problem. He asked George to get one of the coal baskets in the back yard and go down to the river and bring him a basket of water. The basket was completely covered with black dust from the coal mine. George took the basket and went down to the river to fetch the water. When he got back home on the top of the hill, there was no water in the basket. He said, "Grandpa, there is no water in the basket," but the old man told him to do it again. Out of respect for him, George ran back down the hill and dipped the basket in the river then started back up hill to his grandfather. Again, when he got there, there was no water in the basket, but again grandpa said to go back down and get him some water using the basket.

After trying a few times to accomplish this impossible task, George finally gave up. He made it back up the hill one last time totally out of breath holding the empty basket in his hand. Trying to catch his breath and regain his composure, George looked at his grandfather and said, "Grandpa, it is impossible to fetch water in this basket. By the way what does this have to do with the question that I asked you?" Grandpa looked at George and said, "Everything." He then directed him to look at the basket. George looked at the basket and realized that the dirty basket was washed clean. The old man in his wisdom said, "Son, it may not seem like you are getting anything out of going to church but you are. It is gradually cleaning you up even though you don't realize it."

The lesson here is exactly what I believe high school does to you. You may not see it right now, but it is making you a better person. It is preparing you for the life you are going to have when it is all said and done.

My godmother (Agnes Bowman) who just passed away at fifty-four years old once told me that no education is wasted, that one day I will find use for the things that I have learned. I thank her for her wise counsel.

Now Is the Time To Prepare

I was sitting on a bus 5:45 p.m. one Saturday morning on my way to a one-day financial seminar. When everyone got on the bus, just before we started our journey the leader of our group got up and said,

"If anyone is not here, please put your hand up." Without realizing what they were doing, a few people put their hands up but quickly pulled them back down after thinking about the statement for a moment. The truth is there are a lot of people walking around our world today but are really not here. They are not here because they are not prepared for the world that they find themselves in. They may be present physically but are absent in every other way.

I am convinced that if you are in a place in your life and are not prepared to be in that place, it is the same as not being there at all, it would have been better if you hadn't come. It is a tragedy to complete this stage of life and enter adulthood and realize that you are not ready to be an adult.

One of the most frustrating things I have experienced is being improperly dressed for a business meeting. I showed up for this meeting ready mentally, I was emotionally there, but I wasn't properly dressed. We were supposed to be dressed in our business attire even though the meeting was informal. However, when I got to the door, not to mention the fact that I was accompanied by a guest, we were not allowed in because we did not have on the proper attire. What I am trying to say is that preparation is an important part of being successful. Therefore, you must know that just showing up does not guarantee victory. However, to be victorious, you will be required to prepare for it.

> "Opportunity has the uncanny habit of favoring those who have paid the price of years of preparation."
>
> —Unknown Author

To Be at My Best

My good friend Wulwyn, whom I spoke of earlier, was an excellent basketball player. He was also an exceptional leader, and his commitment to the team and to the game was second to none. Because of his attitude toward the game of basketball and his desire to be the best, he excelled above all others. On and off the court he was a very reliable gentleman.

My fondest memory of him as it concerned the game was watching him deny himself the contemporary pleasures of our high school years for the sake of being the best leader and player he could be. When Wulwyn was a senior, I was a junior. During that year, it seemed like there was a party going on every weekend. Basketball and partying were the two things that consumed all of our time outside of the classroom. Some of us hung out all the time it seemed. We were at every party, between parties and having parties of our own. We were equal opportunity partiers. We partied before games, after games, and if it were possible, we would have partied during games.

This was not the case for our captain and the best player on our team. He discriminated whenever the parties interfered with his preparation for games. It was more important for him to be at the top of his ability come game day. Back then I really didn't get it but I do now. This young man that I speak of went on to becoming one of the best basketball players in the history of our school. He also won an award for one of the best people in my life. We remain great friends to this day.

The lesson here is that there has to be something in your life that is worth more to you than the passing pleasures and fads of today. There has to be something you want out of life that is so valuable to you that you will use the time that you now have to prepare to be at the top of your game when that time comes. You will have that big day, that big game, later on in your life that you need to be prepared for, and high school is one of the ways you get ready for the big one. Remember, you do not win just because you showed up. You must be ready to compete, and to compete at a high level, you have to bring your best.

Smaller Things, Bigger Life Meaning

Many times, in life, the smaller, less significant experiences lend great meaning to the more important ones. If you pay attention to the way you conduct yourself in situations that in the larger scope of things may be less important, you will learn a valuable lesson on how you need to conduct yourself when it counts the most.

Take this situation for an example. Let's say that you are preparing for a prom. Think about the level of preparation that is necessary for your event to be successful. Usually, lots of time is spent picking out the perfect dress or the right suit. Young ladies go to great lengths to get the nails and hair right, and young men spend a considerable amount of money on a flashy limousine. All of this is done for a one day event. As a matter of fact, it lasts for just a few hours. Why is it that for a momentary occasion you will spend money, time, and energy? The reason is because you want to be at your absolute best. You want to look your best, you want to ride the best, and be on your best behavior. If the same care is taken to prepare for a grander occasion that is your future, which will last more than just a few hours, you can rest assured that when that day comes you will be at your best.

> "We should all be concerned about the future because we will have to spend the rest of our lives there."
>
> —Charles F. Kettering

It is rather unfortunate that too many young people today spend too much of their time on the now instead of their future. One of the purposes of this book is to help you to focus on the bigger, brighter future that is yours for the taking, but you will have to want it enough to go after it with all you've got.

Hard Work Versus Talent

"Here's a stubborn truth
On which you can bet
The harder you work,
The luckier you get."

—L.J. Huber

In the 2003–2004 NBA season, we saw the unlikely challengers Detroit Pistons square up against the mighty Los Angeles Lakers. The last three years leading up to that year, the Lakers ran off with the titles. They had the superior talents in the league. Not only did they have two of the best players in the history of the game, they also had one of the best coaches in all of basketball. After winning three in a row and making it back to the finals with the best record, that season was supposed to be theirs. But winning the championship was only going to happen for the Lakers if the Detroit Pistons had nothing to say about it.

As a die-hard Lakers fan, it hurts me to say that my team came into the final totally unprepared. They may have thought that they were entitled to win. They thought that just by showing up Detroit was going to roll over and hand them the trophy. I watched the LA Lakers get outplayed, outhustled, and outperformed. I watched hard work dominate talent. I saw desire overtake ability. The world witnessed the knowledge to win take a backseat to the will to win. My Lakers nearly got swept by a group of men who were not as talented as they were, but was willing to work harder for what they desired the most.

I submit to you today that being talented is not enough. I haven't come across a young man or young woman in high school or otherwise that wasn't full of talents and great potentials. Lack of talent is not your challenge; rather, lack of hard work is where you are losing the battle. Someone once said that you can do more with one that has marginal talents but is willing to work than you can with one that has abundant talent but is not willing to put in the work.

Celebrity is huge in our world especial among the younger generation. Have you ever thought about what makes those celebrities so good at what they do? They say that for every glory there is a story. Do you know the story behind Lebron James's success? Read about Beyoncé's work ethics. Learn about the countless hours she spends perfecting her craft. Pick any one of the top performers from any profession; you will quickly discover that they work harder than most of their counterparts. That's what sets them apart from the pack.

What I need you to know is simply this. No matter what you decide to do with your life, if you are not willing to commit to working hard on that thing, it will not yield the kind of fruit that you hope for. My regional vice president Sonia Ashley once said that the way you do anything is the way you do everything. High school is a good place to develop the habit of working hard. If you can begin to work hard on the classes you have right now, even though you may not like them very much, imagine how hard you will be willing to work when you start doing the things that you love to do.

The Power of the Seed

"Luxury is building tomorrows,
living todays, and cherishing yesterdays."

I am convinced that the life you have is a seed given you, complete with all its potentials for the purpose of making all of your dreams come true and fulfilling your purpose here on earth. This statement is most true as it relates to people in their youth, you that are reading this book.

Your youth is a gift, and in this package, there is in it everything you need to be all that you desire to be. However, in order to unwrap this treasure, you will have to first plant it. The treasure in you can be simply unfolded planted and allowed to grow to maturity. For it to grow, it has to be planted. It has to be taken off the shelf of mediocrity and procrastination, and firmly sown in the soil of your future.

I spoke with a bright young man named Matthew and his sister a beautiful young lady named Dede. Their parents own a jewelry shop and Dede works in the shop. They are both teenagers. I met them when I went to the store to purchase a watch. I had to wait for Gabriel, their dad to adjust the strap of the watch and set the time and that took a while so I began to talk with Dede and Matthew. Dede then asked me what I did so I proceeded to tell her that I was a writer, in fact I was in the process of writing this book. I told them what the book was about and began to tell them about the power of the seed. They both listened very intently, Dede stopped doing what she was doing and was focused on me like a laser beam. Matthew hung his head down and tilted his ear slightly in my direction as to not miss anything that I was saying. Before long, Gabriel and his wife Mary stopped doing what they were doing to listen also. It was a powerful moment. It was one of the first times that I gave an impromptu speech to an audience of four that had so much power

65

in it. Anyway, I had to leave quickly because I wanted to write about the experience but I did not want to interrupt the flow of energy that was in that room. Mary, the mother, spoke softly and said, "I wish my other son was here." What I basically told them is what I am telling you now. You can have all the things in life that you desire and more if you spend more time cultivating and planting your seed and less time doing other things, it will bring you a harvest beyond your wildest imagination.

Seeds on the Shelf

If you visit any local supermarket, you will find shelves dedicated to seeds packaged in bags ready for cooking. Some of these bags have been sitting on those shelves for months, maybe even years. What intrigues me about the seeds is that if they were taken off the shelves and planted, they would grow. Left in the bags on display nothing happens, they remain dried, bagged up collecting dust. Each and every seed has it the potential to grow but left in the wrong environment growth is impossible. What am I saying? As you consider your life, you need to realize that you have in you the where-with-all to become successful and productive. What's lacking is the right environment. The environment that I speak of is not a natural one. It is a state of mind. It is having the frame of mind that knows that you are special, that you have what it takes to bring your dreams to reality. It is putting those dreams above the contemporary pleasures and fads. It is investing all that you are into doing the things that are necessary to have the kind of future you desire. It is disregarding all the reasons not to do it and doing it anyway. It is realizing that life is greater than where you are and what you have. It is planting your youth today so as to reap the life that you want tomorrow.

Why Some Don't Sow Their Seeds

Some young people are reluctant to sow their seed because the shelf is a comfortable environment. When the seed remains on the shelf in the store or in the cabinet at home, it is in a controlled environment. The temperature is regulated and the right setting is maintained only for the preservation of the seed, not for growth and multiplication. This is indeed a comfortable place to be in. The bad news is that you are given a fixed price ($1.99 per bag), and you are at the mercy of the cook. If you continue on the shelf long enough, you will become someone's meal. All the possibilities and all the potentials, and all the dreams will become history. What should have been will become what could have been. Let this not be your end. Dare to be planted.

When I Am Planted

"There is an infinity of forests in every seed."

When you decide to be planted, you decide to leave your comfort zone. Because of the possibility of realizing your potential and fulfilling your dreams, you step out into the area where the weather is not controlled. You step out into the dirt where it may be very hot or sometimes very cold. In this new environment, it rains and sometimes it storms. In this environment, it may feel like you are losing your life, but hold on because the cold, the heat, the rain, the storm, and the partial decay are the elements that cause the seed to unfold. These elements aid in the unwrapping of the treasure and the release of the stuff that greatness is made of.

There may be some sleepless nights, there may be some parties not attended, there may be some friends lost, but I guarantee you the dream will not elude you.

The most beautiful thing about the seed is that in the seed, there is a plant, and the plant produces many fruits, and in those fruits, there are many more seeds and on and on and on it goes. Every seed that dies does not do so alone. It dies with other fruits and other seeds trapped in it. Conversely, every seed that is planted and weathers the storms of life becomes a tree that produces much fruits and gives rise to many more seeds that can do the same. Your effect on this world is exponentially increased for many generations to come, and the good news is that in the process you get to have all the things you desire, and you get to live the life of your dreams.

Dennis and the butterfly

A fitting way to end this chapter is to share with you a story I read on the internet some years ago. Every time I get an opportunity to speak with young people I share this story with them. It has had such an impact on my life and I hope it has the same on yours.

Dennis was a very excitable fifth grader who loved doing science experiments. To his greatest joy, his science teacher came to school one day and gave each student in the class a caterpillar in a box. They were learning about metamorphosis. The assignment was to watch the insect turn from a caterpillar into a butterfly. Dennis took his box home a kept it in his room next to the window. He inspected the box at least ten times a day to see if any changes had happened. One morning, when he got up for school, he went over to the window to check on his project. This time there was no caterpillar. It had turned into a pupa and was trapped inside of a cocoon. Dennis was very excited and could not wait to get to school to tell his teacher what had happened. The teacher told him to continue the observation until the butterfly emerges. When Dennis got back home that day, he spent his entire afternoon watching the cocoon to see what happens next. For the next few days he would spend long hours just staring at the cocoon. He would even fall asleep right next to the window.

One day while checking on his box, Dennis noticed that the cocoon was moving. He quickly opened the box to get a full view of the emergence of his long-awaited butterfly. He noticed that the young butterfly had made a crack on the side of the encasement and was trying to get out. Dennis was very excited to finally see what had become of the caterpillar. He watched intently not turning aside for he did not want to miss a moment of this long-awaited day. He waited and waited, but it seemed as though the insect was having trouble getting out of the cocoon. Dennis wanted to help the butterfly get out so he reached into the box, took out the cracked cocoon, grabbed a pair of tweezers out of the drawer, and helped the butterfly get out of the case. When the insect came out, his wings were wet and sticky so Dennis ran to the bathroom and got a hair dryer and dried the butterfly. With wings dried and stretched out, it looked beautiful. It was the most beautiful butterfly he had ever seen but it had a problem, it could not fly.

The young man came to school the next day and told his teacher all that had happened. He told him that the butterfly struggled to come out of the cocoon so he helped him by peeling away the casing. He also told the teacher that he used a hair dryer to help the insect dry faster and added that the insect did not fly. The teacher squatted down to Dennis's level and looked him in his eyes and said, "Dennis, your intentions were good and you need to be commended for what you did, but according to that little insect, it was the worst thing anyone could do for him. You see, Dennis, the struggle that the butterfly goes through in the cocoon is good for him. It is the thing that gives him the wing strength that makes flight possible. For you it seemed like it was too much work, but for him it was the right amount of work he needed to fulfill his purpose. That butterfly will never be able to fly because he did not put in the necessary work." At this point, Dennis felt really bad for what he had done, and realizing this, the teacher gave him another caterpillar. He looked up at his teacher and said "thank you" with a big smile on his face. The lad took the box ran out of the classroom. Just before he went through the door, he turned and said to the teacher, "This time he will have to do all his work." The moral of the story is to never take the easy way out, go through the process, put in the time and work required because your flight is depended upon the strength you build in that process. He who flies must first run, he who runs must first walk, and he who walks must first crawl.

Now what?

- Determine to be the one who works hard in every area of your life
- Know that you have all that you need to be successful (seed)
- Invest your seed (your youth) in your future (goals and dreams)
- Bring your "A" game where it counts the most
- Make a commitment to yourself and to the most important people in your life to do your absolute best in all that you do.
- And remember, you are in the game already so you might as well win it.

CHAPTER 5

KNOW THAT FAILURE IS INEVITABLE BUT SUCCESS IS A CHOICE

"No one is ever defeated until defeat
has been accepted as a reality"

—Napoleon Hill

This chapter rests upon the foundation laid in the first two chapters. I am assuming that if you are still reading this book, that you have at least considered applying the wealth of information that preceded this chapter and started to take decisive actions because of it. Everything that will be said here builds upon what has been previously said and it will be more beneficial for you if you have begun to apply some of the suggestions.

We are going to spend some time talking about failure and success. I am convinced that no one wants to be a failure. No one wakes up in the morning and determines to fail at the things he or she does. Everyone wants to succeed in life. We all want to be able to fulfill our goals and dreams. The problem is that most people live lives of failure but expect success to be their reward. What that means is that there is a certain way of life that produces failure and there is another that produces success. John Maxwell in his book *Failing Forward* said that you begin to be successful when you begin to make decisions that lead to success, and the same is true for failure. Think about that for a minute. As a high school or a middle school student, are you making decision that produce failure, or are your decisions leading you upward to a successful future?

I am going to help you understand how to use failure and setbacks to your advantage and how to create success.

You Are Either Going Up or You Are Going Down

I have learned early on in life that there is no room for people who want to stand around. Everybody must keep moving. Some are moving up while others are moving down. Whenever one stops, he begins to go backward. It is much like walking up a slippery slope. If you ever want to get to the top of the hill, you have to keep moving. Another way to describe it is to look at the idea of riding a bicycle. I know that you probably know how to ride a bicycle. Have you noticed that in order to keep the bike on its two wheels, you have to keep it moving? Even the guys who have learned the skill of balancing it without riding can only do it for a relatively short period of time. What I am saying is that unless you are moving in life to a predetermined destination, you are bound to falter and fail.

As you go on in your personal experience, you must keep making good choices and decisions. Remember that there is no place for indecision. If you don't decide to do the right thing, you've already decided to do the wrong thing. If you don't make good choices, create good habits, and develop good behavior, bad ones will automatically set in. My friend Ron King puts it this way, "Establish your habits early, or establish your habits early." Whatever you do, a habit is going to be establish, good ones on purpose or bad ones by default.

Allow me to summarize what I just said and what I am going to say. If you understand nothing else in this chapter, make sure you get this. You do not need to try hard to fail, but success will not come unless you try hard.

One of Life's Common Denominator

Disappointments, setbacks, road blocks, adversities, and even failures are among some of life's most common phenomena. One hundred percent of the world's population has at some point experienced one or more of these. I have come to realize that these challenges come to separate the winners from the losers. It is said that the same sun that melts the wax, hardens the clay. I guarantee you that if you randomly select ten people from the general population tomorrow during the course of your day and interview them about their lives, what you will find most common to them all will be that they all have or had some level of setbacks, disappointments, adversities, or failures. Among the people interviewed, you will also find varying levels of successes. What separates the high achievers from those who don't is usually the way they deal with or respond to these challenges.

So Why Do We All Experience Failure?

People who experience temporary failure or setbacks are people who are trying to do something or go somewhere. In an attempt to acquire a new skill or reach for new heights, failure becomes a very useful tool if it is used to your advantage. As a teenager, there are always new things to do, new skills to accomplish, and new heights to reach. When you experience setbacks or failure on your way to newer and bigger things, you should not allow yourself to become discouraged because you did not get it right the first time. The disappointment teaches you that you are not quite there yet, but it shows you the areas that you need work on, and most importantly, it shows you one wrong way to not do it. Every time a person fails and learns from his or her failure, that person becomes a better person in the area where the failure occurs.

I heard a story some years back about an enthusiastic young manager for a major cooperation. Having an idea to advance his company, he convinced his bosses to invest one million dollars in his novel venture. To say the least, the venture failed and he lost all of the money. The following week, he came to work and began to pack up his stuff because he knew he was going to be fired. The CEO for the company walked by and saw him packing his things in boxes and asked him what he was doing. The young manger said that he knew that he was going to get fired because of the lost he had cost the company. Looking straight into the young man's eyes, the CEO said, "Unpack your things, young man. You haven't lost a million dollars. You have learned a million-dollar lesson and you are that much more valuable to this company."

"What do you mean?" the young man asked.

"I can't fire you because the lesson you have learned has made you a better, smarter manager and I hope that you will not make the same mistake again. More than that, if I did let you go, I will have to hire another manager who may come in the make the same mistake you made. You are now worth more than a million dollars to us. Get back to work". The lesson here is simple but very profound. Every time you fail at anything in your life and learn from it, you become a better person and your value goes up. This is one truth in life that

I am encouraged by because I am always trying new things and every time I do, I fail a few times before getting it right.

How Do I Get Good?

I am persuaded that it is hope that keeps people alive. Hope for a better tomorrow hope that things will get better, hope that you are going to do better the next time around. Hope allows us all to wake up day after day expecting that today will be better than yesterday. We all want to be and do better. The thing is, in order to get better or be good at the things that we do, you will first have to be bad. "Hold on," you say. "I do not want to be bad. I want to be good at the things I do." We all do, but to be good, you have to start somewhere and that place is right where you are right now. To get good, you have to first be bad, and to be bad you have to try and keep trying. The more you try and fail at becoming good at the things you want to do, the better you become at that thing.

So if you are having trouble in any area of your high school experience (academics or others), my encouragement to you is to keep on trying. It may not seem like it right now, but the truth is you are getting better. Learn from your failures and grow.

I Must Learn to Walk

I have a daughter named Chayil. She is the most beautiful child I have ever seen and I love her more than anything in the entire world. When Chayil was learning how to walk, she like many children exhibited an uncanny desire that will not be satisfied by anything other than her mastering the noble art of walking. In her attempt to conquer her inability to walk she fell many times. Whenever she was able to take a few steps, she would get so excited that she would start to run and the running ultimately ended in a fall. But that did not stop her. Chayil must have fallen about a hundred times. One day she got up on her own and started to take a few steps toward me. I was sitting on the floor in the living room and between us was a stone coffee table. I watched her as she struggled to put one foot in front of the other. I then decided to encourage her and cheer her on to complete the journey to me. As I cheered her on, she got a little bold and took off running. She had a big smile on her face with her hand slightly raised as she made her way towards me. I saw the fall coming but from where I was, there was little I could do about it. Even as I write about it, I can still feel the pain that I felt that day when I helplessly watched by baby girl fall face first onto the stone coffee table. The impact busted her face open, and by the time I got to her, she was screaming at the top of her lungs with blood running down her face. I did all I could to comfort her but the pain was too much to bear so she cried for about of an hour.

The fall left Chayil with scars on her face that took months to go away, but it was not enough to stop her from perfecting the skill of walking. I am proud to announce Chayil walked before the scars even healed. It was almost as if she forgot all about the fall, and focused only on walking I encourage you to do the same.

This story teaches a very valuable life lesson. As you make your journey through life, you may experience some major failures, but I want to encourage you to be like Chayil and never give up. Do not let anything stop you from accomplishing the things in life that are important to you. You may suffer a sever fall, you may be banged up and bruised, and have to scars to prove it but do not let anything stop you from accomplishing your life's goals. Be like Chayil and become an expert at what you want to do. Focus only on what you want.

You have the right to stumble

Have you ever realized that stumbling is act reserve only for those who are moving? People who are going nowhere do not enjoy the benefits of stumbling. Yes, there are benefits in stumbling. I will prove it to you soon. When I speak of stumbling I speak mostly in a figurative sense but it can also be looked at literately.

First let's look at this concept naturally. Stumbling is an action reserved for those who are either running, walking, skipping, or jogging. If you are simply standing still, you cannot stumble. If you lose your balance for some odd reason and hit the ground, you just fell. When you hit the ground, you are either in the same spot where you were standing or you are very close to it.

People who stumble, on the other hand, do not end up in the same spot when they hit the ground. When a person stumbles and falls while in motion, that person falls a few feet forward. They usually have to look back at the thing that tripped them.

Now let us look at the figurative meaning of all this. As you set your life goals and begin to make progress toward their fulfillment, you will undoubtedly experience some stumbling blocks along the way. When you stumble, I want you to know that it is not a total setback. You need to know that even that has caused you to make some advancement. When you look at your surroundings, you should see that you are farther down the road then when you first stumbled.

These are the benefits of stumbling. (1) It is evidence that you are going somewhere, (2) it helps to keep you alert, and (3) it advances you.

Choose To Be a Success

"Always bear in mind that your own resolution
to succeed is more important than any other one
thing."

—Abraham Lincoln

The major difference between the successful people in the world and
those that are failures is simply a choice. Most of what anyone needs
to be successful is available. What separates those who succeed from
those who do not is that those who succeeded decided to be successful. It is that simple. Let us define success. According to most
dictionary success is achieving a desired outcome or accomplishing
an objective. I like to define success as ending up in the place or
with the thing that one desire to end up with. If this is right, then
the responsibility to succeed rests on the person who sets a goal and
desires a certain outcome. I recently came across a quote by Elaine
Maxwell that captures the heart of what I am trying to say here, and
it reads as follows:

> "My will shall shape the future. Whether I fail
> or succeed shall be no man's doing but my own.
> I am the force. I can clear any obstacle before
> me or I can be lost in the maze. My choice, my
> responsibility; win or lose only I hold the key to
> my destiny."

No one can determine the destiny of another. We all hold the
power to make of our lives whatever we want. This should be a great
encouragement to you and should give you a sense of empowerment.

When I first learned that I control my destiny and that I can accomplish any goal that set I to accomplish, I felt a great deal of power come over me. I then began to plan my live and shape my future to reflect exactly what I desire. It was that day that I decided that failure was not an option and that success was my only goal.

One of my favorite writer and speaker is John Maxwell. I own many of his books, taped presentations, and DVDS. He is like a personal mentor and coach to me even though we have never met. I learned the greatest lesson on success from him through one of our many coaching sessions. I do not remember if it was a book or an audio or a video presentation, but the lesson I learned was that, success is not a destination but that it is a journey. He said that I began the journey of success when I begin to make decisions that produce success. It is like the small steps of success in the direction of greater success on a successful journey. The minute I begin to make the kind of decisions that leads one to success, at that very minute, I begin to be successful.

In other words, the successful future that you desire begins right now. It starts with the very decisions that you are making at this very moment. It was you who dreamt of being a doctor or a lawyer or an Oscar-winning actor or a Grammy-winning singer or an NBA or NFL star. Are you making the requisite decisions that will ultimately create the kind of future you desire? No matter what it is that you want to be or do, you will have to start taking the baby steps now in order to get what you want. Every success comes with a price and that price includes hard work, determination, perseverance, and focus.

Create a Habit of Success

"Winning is a habit, unfortunately, so is losing."

—Vince Lombardi

As you travel the road of success, you create a habit of success. You build for yourself a history of little victories that will later serve as an encouragement when you are faced with future obstacles. Every step in the right direction is a step away from the wrong direction. Every time you succeed, you increase your appetite for more success and, subsequently, increase also your distaste for failure. No one becomes a failure or a success overnight. Success and failure are both a result of habit forming. The more you practice one or the other, the more ingrain it becomes in your personality. Create habits of success, and success will be your constant companion.

There was a dog racer who was very famous for predicting the outcome of the race that he put on as a spectacle at the state fair. He had two dogs that he raced all the time, and on any given day, he could confidently predict which dog would win the race. One day after doing this for so many years, a curious spectator asked him how he knew which dog will win every time. His answer was, "I know this because they are my dogs, and prior to the race, I would feed one and not the other." The dog that he fed was stronger than the other. So the one that was not fed always lost the race. Feed your success and you will reap success. Feed failure and you will reap failure.

There Is Nothing Ordinary About Success

Have you ever considered the successful people in your life? Maybe they are your relatives or your friends or maybe it's just someone you see often but with whom you do not have a relationship. Let's take this a step further. What celebrated star do you admire? It really doesn't matter the area of expertise. Is that person a sports star, a musician, a movie star, a talk show host, a doctor, or a lawyer? How about the other successful people you know that are not celebrities— your teachers, your coaches, your parents, their friends, or maybe your neighbor across the street? If you look carefully at the lives of each of these people, there is one thing you will find that is not common to that general population. You will find that these people do things that the ordinary people refuse to do. They go the extra mile so to speak. They invest time and energy in honing, harnessing, and growing their craft.

It is often said that winners dare to do things that loser won't do. Ordinary people sleep too long, watch TV one hour too long, play one hour too long, stay up on the phone talking and texting an hour too long, and spend too much time with the ordinary crowd. It is usually true that the larger the crowd, the more ordinary its makeup. I am sure that you have heard that birds of the same feathers flock together. If the former and the latter statements are true, then it may also be true that one can figure out who and what you are by looking at the kind of people you surround yourself with and the size of that crowd. Are you among the ordinaries or are you one of the few extraordinary? The difference between the ordinary and the extraordinary is the little "*extra*."

The ordinary student does his or her homework and spends the regular time studying. The extraordinary student spends an extra hour after doing the regular, reading over the next chapter, doing one more math problem, adding one final paragraph to that term paper. It is safe to say that all want to succeed, but not all want to do the things that successful people do. So in order to move from the field of the ordinary to that of the extraordinary, all you have to do is a little more than the ordinary crowd is doing.

Slight Shift

When I played basketball in high school, I was not very good from the foul line. My free throw percentage was lacking. I worked on them very hard before after and between practices. I remember my coach coming over to one day while working on my shots. He said that he had been watching me for a while and that he noticed that I was not off by much. He suggested that if I could only shift the ball slightly to the left that I would improve my percentage. From that moment on, all I focused on was making the slight shift, and sure enough, I got better and my free throw percentage went up. In life, the difference between hit and miss is usually a small margin off to the left or to the right. What I am trying to say is that in all areas of your life right now as a high schooler that needs to improve, you only need a slight adjustment to get better. A minor change in the way you are doing things right now can move you from a C to a B, from failing to passing, from losing to winning. The success you are looking for is only a small tweak in your attitude, habits, practices, and character—not a dramatic transformation.

Behind Every Glory There Is a Story

From entertainment, to athletics, to writers, to businessmen, to television personalities, or even presidents, there are many famous people in our world. No matter which famous person you look at, there are a couple of unseen common threads that make their fame possible. Show me a successful person and I will show you a person who has overcome major obstacles, setbacks, and failures. Show me a successful person and I will show you a person who works hard on his or her trade than most.

Most of the time, when young people appreciate a celebrity, they only consider the on-screen glory that that celebrity enjoys. This is the glory that you seek when you idolize that person. What you need to stop and consider is the work that it took for that person to become what you see on TV. If you ever got an opportunity to talk to a famous person about how much time and effort they invest in their craft, you will be amazed to find out how much time and work goes into being who they are. Most successful people work harder than ordinary people. They are up at odd hours of the night, not talking to friends on the phone or playing video games, but doing the things that will make them better at what they do. Many young women admire Beyoncé and will like to have what she has. The real question is: Are you prepared to work as hard as she works? Can you endure the countless number of hours she spends working in the studio, perfecting a song, working on a dance routine? Can you do as many performances as she can? Don't answer yes to that. The bottom line is that behind her glory, there is an unbelievable amount of sweat and tears unimaginable to you and I. The unseen story is what makes it possible for any successful person to have the glory that shines brightly in the public eyes. If you want the glory, you have to be willing to pay the price that is required in order to stand on the pedestal of success and fame. No matter what it is that you want to succeed at, paying the price is the one inescapable element that you must have.

Now What?

Decide right now if you want to be ordinary or extraordinary. The only difference is the "extra." If an extraordinary life is what you choose for yourself, be prepared to go above and beyond what is required. Remind yourself that only those who move stumble, so get moving in the direction that leads you to the completion of your goals. Next, keep in mind that the stumbling you encounter is part of your story, but no one person attained their success alone. Reach out to those who have experience in what you are trying to accomplish. Spend time with those key people in your life that will keep you focused and encouraged. Research how to get better at your craft, and before long, your stumbles will become a confident stride.

CHAPTER 6

KNOW THE PRINCIPLE OF THE AGGREGATE

There are certain basics that everyone who has ever attended school at any length remembers, and these basics stay with us for the rest of our lives. Such basics include the Alphabet song, the nursery rhymes, the days of the week, the months of the year, and the simple addition and multiplication. You will find that many of the things you learn in high school or even in college will not be remembered, but these basics will always be with you.

I want to draw your attention to the basic math that you have learned, particularly addition, and from this, I like to offer the follow principle as stated above in order to explain a life lesson that I believe is most critical as you prepare to leave high school and enter the next phase of your life.

I call this the Principle of the Aggregate. You have to understand that life is about the sum. Everything anybody does is done because of a particular end, which for the sake of this lesson we are going to call the Aggregate or the Sum. Life is not about how you start; it is about how you finish. It is not about where you have been; it is about where you end up. When the all of your life is tallied, what it adds up to is what you should be more concerned about. The outcome of anything is why people do what they do. When a builder builds a house, he is not looking for bricks and steel— he is looking for a building. When a woman conceives, she is looking forward to a baby. Nothing short of a baby will do. You go to school for the diploma; the worker goes to work for the check.

Whether you realize it or not, your life has been adding up, and one day the sum of it all will be evident. I am of the opinion that some of the most important decision you will make in your life, which will for the most part determine the course your life will take, will be made in the next few years. Between your sophomore year in high school and until you graduate college (this is also true for those who don't go to college) every decision you make and every choice you make bears major consequences regarding the outcome of your life. Before now, the choices you made were less weighty, but now life is beginning to take form, and all your decisions matter more than they did just a year or so ago.

What you want or what you are working toward is not what you have now. What you are working toward is what your decisions today are going to produce. That is why I call it the Principle of the Aggregate. We all know that one plus one equals two. No matter how you look at it, one plus one can never give you three. The sum of one plus one is two in America, in Europe, in Africa, in Asia, and everywhere else in the world; and the reverse of that is also true.

Take this for example, years of smoking equal health problems and in many cases cancer. That is a fact and it's even written on the cigarette packs. If smoking was killing people instantly with the first draw, no one would smoke. The reason why many people continue to smoke is because the sum of many years of smoking is not right before their eyes, even though in the back of their minds they know it. The outcome of life is just like smoking. Just like one plus one equals two, so also bad choices plus bad choices equal a life of failure. Many young people continue to make bad decisions because the outcome of their decision is not presently evident. Believe it or not, the choices you make today are determining the future you are going to reap. The more you make the wrong choice or choices that do not support a successful future, the more resolute your failure becomes.

It is safe to say that no one predetermines in their mind to be a failure, but whether a person fails or succeeds is not a matter of will but a matter of action. What you do today is a clear indication of what your tomorrow will look like.

I heard a quote years ago that said that you should be more interested in your future because there is where you are going to spend more time. Unfortunately, young people are too caught up in the present with little concern about the future. Many are in the process, making decision for now, not realizing that those decisions are shaping your future. Everything you are now doing will add to the life that you will inherit. Therefore, you are building your tomorrow today. My question to you is, considering all things you are currently involved in and doing, are you building a future of success or of failure? You should take some time and think about this because what becomes of your life will be the direct result of all the actions you are currently taking. Your life is your responsibility and the outcome of it will be yours as well. You will not be the result of a system or a failing school or a community. You will be the result of your choices so choice wisely.

The Deceptive Nature of Failure

I would like to recommend to you an amazing book called *The Slight Edge*, which is a great complement to this chapter. When I read this book, what I got out of it is that failure as well as success is very deceptive. Dr. John Maxwell said, one begins to be successful when he or she begins to make successful decisions, and this is also true for failure. Success is not a destination. It is process that begins when one starts to make decisions that lead to success, and failure is accomplished the same way.

Failure is, therefore, the result or the sum of many wrong choices made over a protracted period of time. The deception lies in the length of time it takes for the result of your decisions to manifest. In some cases, it may take years, but rest assured that it will surely come. It will not fail. Do not be deceived into thinking that you can just continue doing the things that do not lead to a successful life and maybe some how it will all workout for your good. It never works that way. The fruit of your life will undoubtedly be determined by the seeds that you are currently planting. Consider the following quotation from an unknown source:

> "Excellence is never an accident. It is always the
> result of high intention, sincere effort, intelligent
> direction, skillful execution, and the ability to see
> obstacles as opportunity."

Take a look at the people you have around you today—your close friends, classmates, and other associates. You all may look to be on the same level at this point in time, going in the same direction and doing the same things, but the reality is you are not. In a few short years, the evidence of the decisions everyone is making will soon begin to direct your lives. Many of your peers' lives will begin to turn and show signs of going downward toward a life of failure and unrealized potentials while a few in that number will start to take a slight turn in the upward direction toward success. In a few more years, if each group continues on the same path, there will be a large almost-unbridgeable divide between them as one continues to move further down and the other further up. This happens as a result of what I am going to call "the compound effect of choices."

What I would like you to do at this point is examine the decisions you are making, and if those decisions are leading you downward, stop, turn, and begin to choose differently, but if your decisions are leading you upward, continue to do them with more passion and do not allow yourself to be persuaded otherwise.

> "Everything you are going to be, you are becoming right now."

The above quote is a constant reminder for me to weigh and examine the decisions and choices I make on a monthly basis to ensure that I am becoming what I want my life to be. What you are going to be on a larger scale is what you are creating at the present moment with all the choices you are making. If you become successful, it will be because of the successful decisions you are making today. Your choices are the building blocks that create the life you will ultimately have, but the emergence of what you are constructing takes time to manifest itself. Because of this singular fact, many are deceived to thinking that the wrong decisions they are making over and over will have no consequence on the outcome of their lives. Be assured, however, that the outcome of your life will be determined by the compounding effect of the choices you are making at this very moment and it will happen over a period of time.

Time is the operative word here and it can serve either as your greatest ally or your worst enemy. Since the creation of your destiny takes time and is not determine by a singular act or decision, you may still have time in your favor to stop making harmful decision and begin picking alternatives that support your greatest good. You may also be deceived in thinking that because failure hasn't fully manifested yet that you have time to continue doing what you do even though you know that it is not working for your greatest good.

Have you ever heard this statement "practice makes perfect"? I submit to you that practice does not make perfect. Practice makes better. If you play sports you will find that with practice you become better at that particular sport and not so much at the ones that you do not practice. I grew up playing basketball, and the more I played it, the better I became at the game. I never became a perfect basketball player. There are no perfect people at anything. The point I am trying to make is that if you practice making good decisions now, you will become better at doing it, and with time those choices will yield a life of success, but if you do the opposite, you also will become good at it and when you desire to change course after the undesirable product begins to show up it will be even harder because you would have become experienced at make wrong choices. The more skilled you are at doing anything, the harder it is to do the opposite. With the repetition of any action or choice, you create a habit, and habits, once created, are not easily done away with. Consider the following from an unknown author:

> Who am I?
> I am your constant companion,
> I am your greatest helper or
> your heaviest burden.
> I will push you onward or drag
> you down to failure.
> I am at your command.
> Half of the task that you do
> you might just as well
> Turn over to me and I do them
> quickly and correctly.

I am easily managed; you merely
need to be firm with me.
Show me exactly how you want something done.
After a few lessons, I will do it automatically.
I am the servant of all great people
And the regret of all failures as well.
Those who are great, I made great.
Those who are failures, I have made failures.
I am not a machine but I will
work with all its precisions
Plus, the intelligence of a person.
Now you may run me for profit
or you may run me for ruin.
It makes no difference to me.
Take me, train me, be firm with me
And I will lay the world at your feet.
Be easy with me and I will destroy you.
I am called habits.

There is no time in your life that is more important than right now to begin to create the habits that will lead to the creation of the life that not only blesses you but the world at large.

"The harder you are on yourself,
the easily life will be on you."

—Ron King
Primerica Life Insurance Company

Life has a tendency of treating favorably people who, for the purpose of accomplishing a certain goal, exercise a level of self-imposed restriction particularly pertaining to contemporary pleasures.

If your desire for a bright future outweighs your desire to indulge in the pleasures of today, life will produce for you a future that many who overindulge present-day enjoyment will never have.

Another very powerful way to better understand the above quote is to consider the life of the celebrities you may or may not love. If study the life of any of the greatest, most popular celebrity the first and most obvious thing that might jump out at you will be their lifestyle: the glamour, the fame, the money, and so on. But what you will not notice at first glance is the price that had to be paid in order for them to be where they are. Take Michael Phelps for example. The most celebrated Olympian of all time. This one individual has more gold medals than anyone in the history of the world. Now we know him, we know his face, we see the glory and the accolades. What we don't see is all the work it took for him to be the world greatest Olympian. He has spent more time in the water than most young men his age will ever do. He spent many long hours practicing and perfecting his craft. I can imagine him foregoing countless "fun" events because he had to go to practice or get ready for an important meet. Setting time goals in each event that he participated in, reaching those goals, and then setting new ones, I imagine this to be his life prior to being the great Olympian we now know. This was all done because there was something he considered more important than current pleasures. The point I am trying to make is that in order for you to be successful on any level and achieve highly at anything, there has to be a certain degree of self-imposed discipline and sacrifice. You have to be committed to paying the price now for the life you wish to have later.

A Predetermined End

The principle of the aggregate works whether you know it or not, but there is one very important ingredient of this rule that allows it to work in your favor and for your greatest good and that is "having a predetermined end." Let me explain. As you close this chapter of your life and open the next, you will be faced with many tough yet attractive choices (the good, the bad, and the ugly), and because you at this time in your life will be entering adulthood, being the one with whom the final judgment for all your decisions is made, if you are not equipped with a predetermined end or a personal vision for the outcome of your life, you may find yourself tossed to and fro by every wind of change, not making any significant progress. Having a personal vision for your life puts you in a better position than most who don't. It allows you to focus your time, talents, and energy. It determines the way you spend your time and with whom you spend it. The end in mind, which is another way to call it, will direct your energy. It will tell you what you should or should not do, where you should and should not go. You wouldn't need the pressure of an external authority nor would you succumb to the beguiling distractions that are contrary to the end you seek. It will bring to you the right people, lead you to the right places, and cause you to have the right experiences all for the sake to getting you to end you desire.

Without a predetermined end, the principle still remains in effect, only this time your life will go in circles, in and out of varying experiences, with different types of people in many places, not adding up to much. People like this, spend more years in college than they should, too long in the wrong relationship, and don't make many, if any, significant contributions to society. Having an end firmly planted in your mind will speed you past all the popular enticements that pull others under their spell and lead you straight into a great future.

From this point on, I want you to begin to see your life as a construction project. I have spent many years in the field of construction, and any builder will tell you that one of the fundamental things to have before a project begins is the building plans. The building plan is in actuality the completed building on paper or as conceptualized. With the end product, the builder can now begin to construct, one brick at a time, based on the plans and eventually the building that was once only on paper emerges. As a matter of fact, many construction projects have actual pictures of the finished building a long time before the process begins. The plans dictate the type of materials that are used, the kind of equipment that are needed, and the details that are required to create exactly what the plans call for. This is possible only because there was a plan to follow, there was an end in mind.

Permit me if you would and play a bit of a mind game with me. Come with me as we visit a construction site that we both know and have seen many times. This project is the project of your life and you have been given full responsibility to oversee the process from start to finish. But all that you have is an empty piece of land; however, you have a very limited time to construct a house on it. You come to this project with limitless resources, abundant support, but no plans. How are going to know where to start? What tools are you going to use? What resources are you going to employ? If you attempt to do anything without first securing a plan, you will end up with a disaster. Yet many are attempting to build a life without a plan. As you read this book, I encourage you to figure out what it is that you want to do with your life. Determine what you want the outcome of your life to be. Get, if you can, a picture of what that outcome looks like, then go out and begin to build it, one brick at a time, always keeping in mind the finished product and always making all decisions in consultation with the original plans.

The presence of materials and equipment on a construction site is evidence that a building is in progress. The presence of bridge building equipment and materials are evidence that a bridge is in progress. When your life is considered, let the presence of the equipment, materials, and the work that is being done be the evidence that a great life is in progress.

Make Decisions Consistent with the Future You Desire

From the minute you were born until the day you leave this earth, you will be making decisions and choices. Every decision you make has consequences, and the consequences for the decisions that you are going to be making in the next few years of your life may last a lifetime. That is why it is very important that you understand this fact. Earlier on in your life when you chose your favorite color, your favorite food, or the type of hair style you preferred, you were exercising your right and ability to make your own choices and to decide for yourself, but that right and ability has the potential to either serve you or destroy you if you do not use it wisely. Making those earlier decisions did not carry the weight and consequences that the ones that you are about to make at this stage of your life. This is why I believe that there is no more important time in your life than right now when it comes to directing your life into the future that you desire and it happens by the choices that you make. The decisions that you make at this stage of your life can and will have lasting impact on the outcome of your life. This book is written to aid you in that process. My hope is that it serves as a guide as you prepare to enter into what is called the real world where real, lasting outcomes follow every decision you make.

At this point in your life, every choice you make whether small or great has the power to form the direction of your life and the ultimate outcome of your future, especially if you are going to be making the same choice repetitiously. Every decision, good or bad, is harder the first time you make it, and it is invariably followed by others that support the first and are easier to make. By repeating similar decision, you create a pattern or a habit, and a history of a habit creates a life. If you want a certain kind of life, you need to first decide what that life is that you desire and then start making choices that will eventually create that life. Every time you make a decision that supports the life you want to build, that choice informs your subconscious, making it easier to make another one like it, and the process turns your life in the direction that you want it to go in. It may seem gradual at first or not having any impact, but keep on making the right decisions and one day your life will shoot up like a rocket into the future you imagined. Every success story happened one decision at a time, and every failed life happened one decision at a time but never right away. Therefore, make decisions now that will create the life that you want and never give up before you see the outcome.

Chasing the Rabbit

One beautiful summer afternoon, a dog is sitting on the front porch of his house taking in the sun and enjoying a quiet rest in nature's bounty. Suddenly, there appeared out of nowhere a bunny rabbit skipping along through the yard. The dog jumped up from his rest and began chasing the rabbit through the neighborhood, barking as aloud as he possibly could. As he chased the rabbit, he went past a second dog also sitting outside on his porch. The second dog heard the loud barks and saw the first dog running, so he too began to chase after the first dog. They both ran and barked very loud. Soon a third dog saw what was going on and he too joined the chase. He chased after the second dog chasing the first dog chasing the rabbit. Not long after, a fourth dog, a fifth dog, and a sixth dog joined the chase.

This created a train of six dogs running and barking loudly through the neighborhood. They zipped past unsuspecting people, over and under hedges, around parked cars, across several streets, even stopping the flow of traffic at certain points. The chase continued for several minutes and it seemed as if it would never come to an end. The sixth dog chased the fifth dog, the fifth dog chased the fourth dog, the fourth dog chased the third dog, the third dog chased the second dog, the second chased the first dog, and the first dog chased the rabbit. At the end of the train dog number six began to think about the purpose of the chase. It didn't seem to make sense to him. All he saw was a group of dogs running and thought it was a good idea so he joined in. The chase quickly lost its excitement for him, so he quit the chase and went back home. The fifth dog started to gradually slow down as he remembered that it was almost lunch time and he was going farther and farther away from home. He also quit the pursuit and headed home. As the remaining dogs continued to run, they went past the home of dog number four. Recognizing his familiar environment, he made a sharp left away from the chase and returned to the place that he was most comfortable. The chase now in its tenth minute slowly started to interfere with dog number three's grooming appointment. Realizing this he too abandoned the hunt and made his way home to be there in time for his grooming session.

The second dog, having been in the chase for the longest except for the first dog, began to reflect on the reason for the chase to begin with. He thought, "I have been chasing this dog that I don't even know for over fifteen minutes but I have no idea what he is running after. Everyone else has left and gone home. It is foolish for me to continue after this crazy dog. I'm going home." So with that, he quit the chase and went home. The chase was back to one dog chasing one rabbit. The first dog continued chasing the rabbit until he caught it. Question: Why did the first dog stay with the chase until he caught the rabbit? Answer: He was the only one of the six dogs that saw the rabbit.

Lesson: As you progress in your life particularly through the next few years, there will emerge many attractive chases in which many will run. My advice to you is not to chase after other people's rabbit but to find your own rabbit because the only rabbit you can catch is the one that you see.

Now What?

Visualize your end. Write it down. Speak it out often to yourself. Use your vision for your future as a measuring tool in your decision-making process. Remember if the friends, choices, places, purchases, and entertainment do not align with what your ultimate end requires, they are just not worth it.

CHAPTER 7

KNOW YOUR
RESPONSIBILITY

For the past eight years of my life, I have had front row seat to the most exciting show I on earth. This show has been watching my kids grow up. Tyrese, Chayil, Nia, and Napoleon (better known as Asher) are putting on a once-in-a-lifetime performance, and I am glad to be tagging along for the ride.

When my kids were born, they had absolutely no personal responsibility. Everything they needed was provided for them, and just about everything they wanted was made available. They were not required to do anything. Someone was always there to meet their every need and desire. Whenever they were hungry, food was made available. How it was made possible, who had to work to earn money in order to purchase the food, or who had to prepare it was none of their concern. All they did was let out a cry and their parents had to figure out if that cry meant "feed me," "change me," "something's hurting me," or "I just want someone to pick me up."

Taking care of our kids was the sole responsibility of ours. At that tender age in their lives, they had absolutely no personal responsibility. As I think about this, it makes me grin a little to know that

God himself, realizing this, did not give infants morning breath or smelly underarms, because He knew that they did not have the ability to clean their mouths or apply deodorant.

Responsibility

According to the dictionary, the word *responsibility* means "a task, duty, or job." I would like to add my personal connotation to the word. For the purpose of this book, let us think of the word as "having the ability to respond properly or correctly to a task, duty, or job." It is clear to see that no one can hold another liable to perform any duty if that person does not have the ability to properly handle that task. The ability to handle any job usually comes by teaching and practice, which is accompanied by physical and mental capabilities.

The laws of the land limits us to certain responsibilities based on those four factors mentioned. Your parents respect this truth and the educational system also acknowledges it. That is the reason why no one goes to college until he or she first finishes high school.

I have said all this to say that, from childhood to now, a little more responsibility will be given to you based on your ability to properly react or respond to each task. For example, when my children were about six years of age, they were responsible for showering on their own, brushing their own teeth, and putting on lotion among other things like making their bed because they had the ability to assume these personal duties. To this point, it would be ridiculous, unfair even to expect my children to earn a pay check, drive to school, or cook their own meals at the age of six.

Responsibility to Self

The first and most important responsibility you have is the responsibility to yourself. Originally, I was going to title this chapter "Know That Your Responsibility Is About to Shift" but I decided against it. The shifting of most, if not all, of the obligation to provide for yourself and to completely manage the affairs of your life is done when you leave high school. For most, working and earning money to meet basic necessities will soon become their duty. You will soon realize that the juice in the refrigerator did not magically appear; it will soon become apparent that the box of cereal does run out and that milk has an expiration date. It will soon be very clear to you that if you do not put it there, it will not show up. Laundry does not just wash itself, beds do not make themselves, and the light will not just stay on if someone is not making it happen. This is just the tip of the iceberg.

More important than taking care of your natural and physical need is the duty of guiding the life in the direction that you want it to go. Without the constant oversight of your parents or guardians, you are now standing at the helm with all the power in your hands to steer your life in the direction that you chose. Whether or not you wake up on time for your classes is all on you; no one will force you to study or do your assignments any longer. Pass or fail, it's all on you. You are the maker of your destiny, the captain of your ship, and lord of your kingdom. You will own every choice from this point on. I admonish you to take seriously the shift that is about to happen in your life and be ready to embrace the challenges ahead. It only gets tougher going forward, but I heard it said that "tough times don't last, tough people do," so when times get tough, don't ask for the burdens to be less. Ask for your shoulders to be wider and stronger. Grow broader and stronger shoulders because after you have carried your responsibilities and fulfilled your life, you will have to carry those of others even if it is just for a short while. At the end of it all, it all comes down to choices and every choice has its consequences. The persistence of one choice or another will magnify the consequence. So chose rightly and chose rightly continually, for in so doing you will create the life you desire.

Responsibility to Others

Now that you hopefully understand your responsibility to yourself, I would argue that your responsibility to others is just as important to understand and to perform. However, the former should always precede the latter because if you do not know and carry out your duty to self, it is impossible to serve others. This is why I lead with thought of you recognizing your responsibility to yourself before going on to discuss your responsibility to others. The very first thought you need to conceive is the fact that you are who you are because responsible people took the time and performed their duties toward you in teaching, leading and guiding you, and creating a world in which you can grow to become all that you imagined your life to be. This thought should then invoke in you a second consideration, which is the remembrance of all the people who have helped shape your life and the sacrifices that it took on their part to do so. An appreciation of those sacrifices should allow you to take your life more seriously.

Having looked back and appreciated the people who impacted your life, let's now look forward and consider your responsibility to the next generation. I do not think that it is too early to begin to think this way. As a matter of fact, I think that the earlier the better and the more prepared you'll be to embrace the task when it comes. You need to embrace the fact that you live in a world that was thought of and brought into reality by visionaries who came before you. Everything you enjoy today was created by people who took seriously their responsibility to fulfill their dreams and to make the world a better place. Today you and I get to enjoy the fulfill-ment of all those dreams. So as you look forward, I encourage you to continue to remind yourself from this point on that you have the responsibility not only to make something of your life but to also help others make something of theirs. As a matter of fact, this book is my way and my attempt to help you become all you can be just like others have done for me. If one life is changed as a result of this book, it would be worth all the time and effort to write and publish it. Allow me to leave this thought with you. Imagine what our world will be like if all the dreams, sweat, and sacrifices were not fulfilled and done. Imagine what that world will look like. In that world, there are no cell phones or even land line phones. In that world, there are no cars, no video games, no Internet, no theme parks, no designer shoes or clothes, no buildings. Without dreamers who labored to bring their dreams to reality, our world will be void of all of those things and more. Our world would be void of most things you take for granted every day. This is the burden that we all bear, the burden to fulfill our dreams and to leave the world a better place than we met it. This is your responsibility to your city, your community, your country, and your world.

"To whom much is given much will be required."

—The Bible

The bicycle metaphor

As we bring this book to a close, I have to leave you with this idea. For many months, I have been fascinated by the process of learning how to ride a bicycle and the actual process of riding one. I had no idea that there was so much written and said about bicycles from the time it was invented in 1817 until now. The bicycle really is a fascinating piece of innovation, and there is a lot about life that one can learn so we are going to be looking at this amazing invention and try to draw some parallels.

Everyone Needs a Spotter

It is probably safe to assume that most, if not all, people who have ever ridden a bike either with the training wheels or without, was helped by someone the first time they tried to ride. A lot of you still have found memories of when you learned to ride and the person who taught you how to ride. Do you remember the time you first rode without training wheels? Remember how afraid you were? Now do you remember telling your trainer to push you but also to hold on and not let you go?

I remember having the same talk with my daughter as I taught her how to ride. I tilted the bike to the side and encouraged her to get on. After she did, I then told her to put her feet on the pedals, look ahead, not down, and to keep the handle bar straight. I then began to push slowly while helping her balance her weight by also holding the handle bar and the back of the seat at the same time. Without my help in balancing the bike and pushing her, she would have fallen right off. But as I pushed her I then began to tell her to pedal and she did. When she gained momentum, I gave her one good shove and let her go. She rode steadily on her own for a few feet with me jogging next to her to make sure that she does not fall and hurt herself badly. We repeated the process a few times and she got better with every other try. The better she got, the farther she rode. She kept her head up, looking straight, she kept pedaling, steadied the handle bar, and made a complete lap around the track on her own. She did it again and again and went faster and faster with every lap. At that point, my

104

job was done; she can ride on her own now. I will never need to teach her how to ride again.

This example is life itself. No one comes into the world with all the knowledge on how to ride this thing called life. We are all taught. That's why you have parents, and teachers, and mentors. They teach you how to get on the bike (life), how to keep our balance, how to pedal, and how to keep looking ahead so that you do not fall. The purpose of a spotter is not to do the work for you. They are there to teach you how, show you how, and help you do it on your own. You can't do anything unless you're taught, you can't be taught unless you have a teacher, and the teacher can't teach unless you are willing to learn.

Take Off My Training Wheels

I failed to mention earlier the bike I taught Chayil to ride belonged to Tyrese. He had outgrown his old bike, so we had to get him a bigger one. Since Chayil had taken interest in riding bicycles, we decided to hand it down to her until she learned how to ride. At first Chayil was concerned that the bike was not pink. Pink was her favorite color. We explained to her that she can have his old bike until she learns how to ride, then we would buy her a pink bike. She remained disappointed until she actually got on the bike and rode it. I remember the very first time my wife and I took the kids to the park to ride their bikes. Tyrese was excited about his new bike, and Chayil was excited about being able to ride. This was her first time riding a bike unassisted so there were training wheels on the back of the bike. That day the kids had a great time, Tyrese being the more experienced rider zooming around the track and Chayil riding for the first time enjoyed every moment of it while trying to keep up with her brother.

Frustration set in when Chayil realized that her training wheels were keeping her from going as fast as Tyrese. She appealed to me to remove her training wheel but I refused. I then tried to explain to her that she needs the wheels because they were there to help her learn to ride. Without the training wheels, it will be almost impossible for a five-year-old to be able to ride a bike for the first time without help. As a matter of fact, that child would be in danger of falling and hurting him or herself. The bottom line is that I could not hold my daughter responsible for not being able to ride a bike before teaching her how to do so. Tyrese, on the other hand, had his training wheels removed because, at eight years old and after practicing for months, he was able to handle riding on his own.

This experience is symptomatic of life in general. Until this point in your life, you have been riding with the training wheels still attached. By the time you leave high school, you are going to be expected to be able to handle many personal responsibilities on your own. A great number of you are going to be expected to be able to stand on your own two feet. The training wheels are totally coming off, and it is time to establish your balance, walk the proverbial road of life, and run your own life as it is sometimes said. My desire is to help you to begin to think in these terms and to get you ready for what lies ahead. When the wheels come off, you will be completely responsible for what becomes of your life. Whether the outcome is good or bad is totally up to you.

You Are the Engine

Up until this point in your life, you have basically been told by the adults who had supervision over you what to do and what not to do. They have been the force and the reason why you are where you are at this point. They have helped you to get started. They got you on the bike, held it as you got on. They held on to the handle and the back of the seat and walked beside you as you practiced how to ride. They have been letting go gradually as you got more confident riding on your own. The time is coming and for some has come when they are going to give you one good push and stand back and watch you ride by yourself. From this point on, you will become the engine, the force that moves the bicycle. Bicycles have no motor, no engine. Unless you pedal, they go nowhere. Unless you move them, they stay in the same place. It is about to be totally up to you to move, to drive yourself and to steer life in the direction that you choose. You are about to be 100 percent responsible for everything that happens in your life the for the outcome of it.

Maintaining Your Balance

"Life is like riding a bicycle. To keep your balance, you must keep moving"

—Albert Einstein

Another crucial aspect of successfully riding a bicycle is maintaining your balance as you travel from one point to the next. It is very difficult to maintain your balance while looking backward or looking down. Looking back can be understood as spending too much time focusing and remembering past failures or even past successes. You should learn from past failures and keep moving forward. Try not to ever get stuck mentally or emotionally as a result of a failure or setback. As you move from one victory to the next, never allow yourself to spend too much time celebrating one victory, or it will have the same impact as spending too much time on failure. Celebrate every success and store it away for future encouragement then move forward for there are more to win and greater successes to be had.

Looking down, however, is indicative of giving too much attention to what is happening right now. Your current situation, your surroundings, your peers, what's happening in pop culture. When you do this, you lose sight of where you are going and naturally increase the risk of running into something.

Always set your focus on what lies ahead, always have the next big thing in mind, always be on your way to the next victory, always be on your way somewhere. Keep moving forward. To maintain your balance at this stage in your life and for many years to come, you must keep moving forward and never stop always keeping in mind your ultimate destination.

Set Measurable Attainable Goals

As the burden of your life shifts more and more on you, you will now be responsible for setting your own goals and making sure that you hit those targets. The time is quickly approaching when no one will tell you what to do with your life or force you to do something you don't want to do. You have to learn now how to set your own goals and work to achieve them. A good way to start the process is to set goals that you can measure and goals that are attainable. By measure I mean, that when you set a goal, there has to be a way for you to determine where you are as it relates to achieving that goal and how to calculate your movement toward your desired result. It is like me working on my free throw percentage, a runner timing his speed, moving up a letter grade in a particular subject and so on. By doing this, you will inspire confidence in yourself and in your ability to achieve that goal. I learned a long time ago that one cannot manage what he cannot measure. If you can measure, then you will be able to make the necessary adjustments on your way to achieving what you want.

Check Your Score

The purpose of a score board is to keep an ongoing record of who's winning and who's losing. Without keeping scores, we are either just practicing or simply playing just to break a sweat. I must submit to you that the world that you are about to inherit is a very competitive world and that everybody is playing to win. This is not a dress rehearsal, this is not practice, and you are not just playing to just break a sweat. This is the real deal. This is the major league, the pros, and if you want to compete on this level, you must bring your "A" game, you must come to win. In this world, there are always winners and losers. I want you to be among the people who get it right, the ones who win, and in order to do that, you must know your score. You must have a clear view of your personal score board as it relates to your goals and dreams. You must always know if you are winning or if you are losing, and if you find yourself falling back, you should stop immediately and begin to make the changes that will get you back on top.

Now

The best way I know how to bring this book to a close is to leave with the idea that everything that has been discussed here will and can only be beneficial to you if they are applied now. There is no better time than now. Not yesterday, not tomorrow, but right now. Now, while the information is fresh in your mind. The best time to utilize new and life-changing knowledge is when you first get it, when the excitement is at its highest. All you have is now. There is no tomorrow if there is no *now*. What you do right now will impact the rest of life. As a matter of fact, all you do have is now. All of your yesterdays were nows when you were in that moment. What you are at this moment is a direct result of what you did with all the moments that you had when they were nows. Everything that is going to become of you will take direct roots in the now that you currently occupy, and when you take action, there will still be a now. Life is a succession of nows, and what happens in all of those moments will influence the result that you will have in the future when that future becomes now. Therefore, your most important moment is now. Take full advantage of what you do now, no matter how much or how little it is because the rest of your life is completely dependent on it.

Thank you.

ABOUT THE AUTHOR

Napoleon Ricks is a husband, father, author, public speaker, and youth leader with over twenty years of experience working with young people nationally and internationally. His many years of work and true desire to impact the next generation is brought together in this book, inspired first by his two teenaged children and by all the young men and women he has worked with over the years. 7 Things You Need to Know Before Leaving High School is his labor of love and service to all teenagers throughout the world, and it is his desire that none leaves high school without reading this book.

CPSIA information can be obtained
at www.ICGtesting.com
Printed in the USA
FSHW012137180919
62155FS